TAOS
Landmarks & Legends

Bill Hemp

TAOS
Landmarks & Legends

Written and Illustrated
by
Bill Hemp

By the same author:

NEW YORK ENCLAVES

Clarkson N. Potter, Inc./Publisher

New York

Distributed by Crown Publishers

IF EVER YOU GO TO DUBLIN TOWN

The Devin-Adair Company

Old Greenwich, Connecticut

Copyright © 1996 by Bill Hemp

Library of Congress Catalog Card Number 95-60832

Printed in the United States of America

ISBN 0-9444 82-40-6 (Paper Trade)

ISBN 0-9444 82-41-4 (Hardcover Trade)

ISBN 0-9444 82-42-2 (Collector's Edition)

Cover and Text design by Brendan Hemp

Composed in Caslon Open Face and Caxton Book

by John Cole Graphic Designer

Edited by Mary Mann

Printed and bound by Thomson-Shore, Inc.

Published by Exceptional Books, Ltd.

Los Alamos, New Mexico

Dedication

FOR MAGGIE

Our Love is a Many-Splendored Thing

Acknowledgements

I wish to thank the following friends, neighbors and townspeople of Taos, New Mexico, and points east without whose genuine interest, cooperation and support this work would not have been written:

Elizabeth and John Allred, Curtis Anderson, Lynn Arany, John Artopoeus, Sally Bachman, Art Bachrach, John Batis, Jack Beimer, Ed and Melissa Bell, Mickey Blake, Dorothy Berninghaus Brandenburg, Jack Brandenburg, Barbara Brandenburg Brenner, Jeff Boyer, Charles Brooks, Audrey Brown, Carol Brown, Don Burnes, Harold Burson, the Kit Carson Museums, Jeff and Jill Caven, Dennis Cesa, Allan Clevenger, Rev. Charles P. Costello, S.J., Beth Couse, Dixie and Don Dickerson, Virginia Dooley, Kit and Ted Egri, Steve Eich, Eya Fechin, Clark Funk, Sandi and Stormstar Gomez, Isaac Gonzales, R.C. Gordon-McCutchan, Char Graebner, Jim Griffin, Margery Hanisee, Stuart Hardy, The Harwood Foundation and Library, Bill Hemp, Jr., Kelly Dietrich Hemp, Rod Hubble, Bill "Cowboy" Jaggers, Eloy Jeantete, Alan and Coralie Jones, Saki Karavas, Rick and Terry Klein, Virginia Couse and Ernie Leavitt, Edwin and Novella Lineberry, Andy and Bobby Lindquist, Stephen Linker, Tal Luther, Bea Mandelman, Vincente Martinez, Tracy McCallum, Kerry McLaughlin, Don and Jean McMahill, Roberta Courtney-Meyers, Dwight Myers, Skip Miller, Carey Moore, Dollie Mondragon, Rosalie Morgas, Jim and Roxanne Murphy, John Nichols, Faye and Otto Noeding, Rose-Marie Packard, Mayor Fred Peralta, Peter Rabbit, Tony Reyna, The Millicent Rogers Museum, Martin Romero, Diana and Livingston Ross, Rev. Edmund Savilla, Deborah Sherman, Corina Santistevan, Alice Shetler, Rick Smith, Gloria Spitz, Dee Strassburg, The Taos County Historical Society, Tom Tarleton, Patty Taylor, Hattie Trujillo, Betty and Joe Tyson, Carmen Velarde, Jenny Vincent, Ben Wade, Barbara and Frank Waters, Eileen and Fred Wendler, Dianne Williams, Ken Winslow, David Witt and Kenna Wood.

I would also like to thank my son, Brendan Collins Hemp, for designing the cover of this book, a work of art in itself.

Last, but certainly not least, I extend my heartfelt thanks to my lovely wife, Maggie Collins Hemp, who lent her support, time, patience, encouragement and love over the past two years of my life—all this while I spent hour upon hour in my greenhouse studio—that she gave to me as a 65th-birthday present, writing these thirty chapters and completing more than 100 pen-and-ink drawings.

To one and all, a sincere thank you!

Bill Hemp
Casa Magpie
Taos Cañon, New Mexico
June 1995

"Who has seen the women,
Heard the bells, or smelled
The *piñón* smoke of Taos
Will never be able to leave."

Kit Carson

"Coronado se paseaba por toda la tierra 'fuera,
Y no hubo quien le pisara el paso de su bandera.
Por aqui', por alli', que bueno va!
Por aqui', por alli', que bueno va."

"Coronado travelled throughout the earth,
And there was no one who could
Follow in those footsteps.
Here and there, here and there,
How good it was!
Here and there, here and there,
How good it was!"

"It had to end in the Taos Valley,
green with trees and fields of alfalfa,
populated by dark-skinned people who
greeted me pleasantly. Then I saw my
first Taos Indians, picturesque, colorful,
dressed in blankets artistically draped,
New Mexico had gripped me . . . ."

Ernest L. Blumenschein
Excerpt from His Journal

Fragment of a Ballad Recited by
Gertrudes S. de Garcia, a Navajo in 1933
at the Age of 110.*

*Hispanic Culture in the Southwest *by Arthur L. Campa,
University of Oklahoma Press, Norman.*

Table of Contents

Table of Contents

Kit Carson

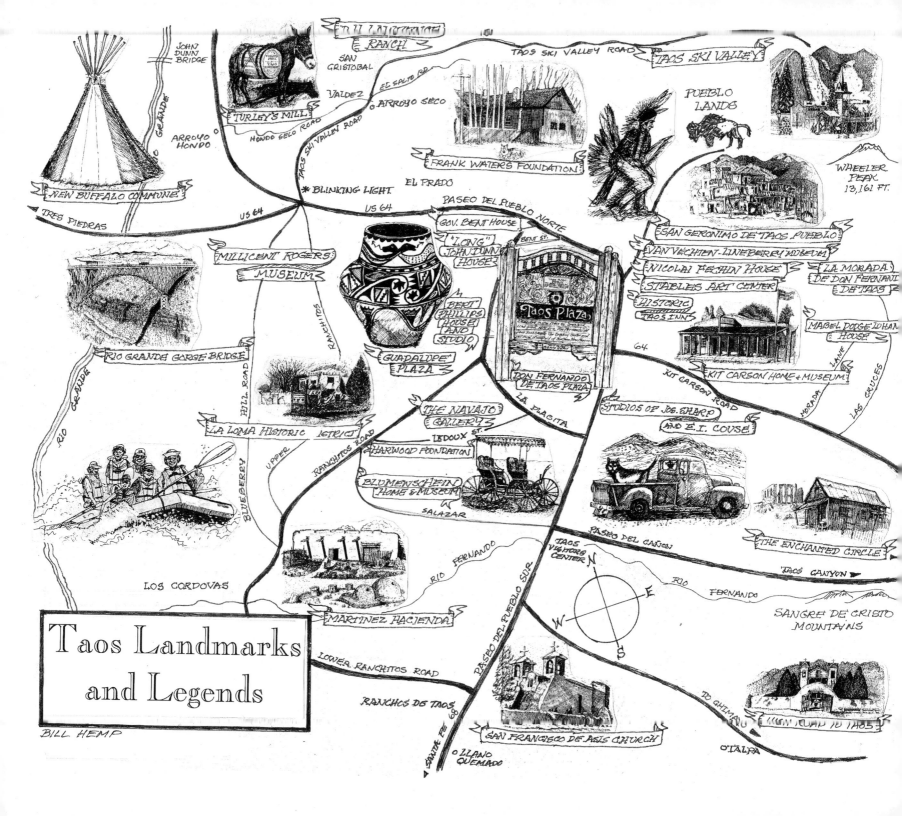

Taos Landmarks and Legends

BILL HEMP

JOHN DUNN BRIDGE

RIO GRANDE

SAN CRISTOBAL

D.H. LAWRENCE RANCH

TAOS SKI VALLEY ROAD

TAOS SKI VALLEY

VALDEZ

EL SALTO RD.

ARROYO SECO

HONDO SECO ROAD

TAOS SKI VALLEY ROAD

PUEBLO LANDS

WHEELER PEAK 13,161 FT.

ARROYO HONDO

TURLEY'S MILL

FRANK WATERS FOUNDATION

NEW BUFFALO COMMUNE

BLINKING LIGHT

EL PRADO

PASEO DEL PUEBLO NORTE

TRES PIEDRAS

US 64

US 64

GOV. BENT HOUSE

"LONG" JOHN DUNN HOUSE

BENT ST.

SAN GERONIMO DE TAOS PUEBLO

VAN VECHTEN-LINEBERRY MUSEUM

NICOLAI FECHIN HOUSE

LA MORADA DE DON FERNANDO DE TAOS

MILLICENT ROGERS MUSEUM

RANCHITOS

BERT PHILLIPS HOUSE AND STUDIO

STABLES ART CENTER

HISTORIC TAOS INN

RIO GRANDE

RIO GRANDE GORGE BRIDGE

HILL ROAD

GUADALUPE PLAZA

Taos Plaza

MABEL DODGE LUHAN HOUSE

64

LA LOMA HISTORIC DISTRICT

UPPER

RANCHITOS ROAD

DON FERNANDO DE TAOS PLAZA

KIT CARSON ROAD

MORADA LANE

LAS CRUCES

KIT CARSON HOME + MUSEUM

RIO GRANDE

BLUEBERRY

THE NAVAJO GALLERY

LEDOUX ST.

LA PLACITA

STUDIOS OF JOS. SHARP AND E.I. COUSE

HARWOOD FOUNDATION

BLUMENSCHEIN HOME & MUSEUM

SALAZAR

PASEO DEL CAÑON

THE ENCHANTED CIRCLE

TAOS CANYON

LOS CORDOVAS

RIO FERNANDO

TAOS VISITORS CENTER

RIO FERNANDO

SANGRE DE CRISTO MOUNTAINS

MARTINEZ HACIENDA

N

W   E

S

LOWER RANCHITOS ROAD

PASEO DEL PUEBLO SUR

RANCHOS DE TAOS

SANTA FE 68

LLANO QUEMADO

SAN FRANCISCO DE ASIS CHURCH

TO CHIMAYO

SAN JUAN DE TAOS

TALPA

INTRODUCTION

Driving north on Highway 68 from Santa Fe, the traveler gears up a horseshoe curve from the Río Grande Canyon onto a high plateau. One is suddenly awestruck by the expansive vista of the Sangre de Cristo Mountains and sagebrush mesa land bordered on the west by a deep river gorge. Together they create the magnificent drama of the Taos Valley.

There on a high desert shelf at an altitude of 6,967 feet, nestle a cluster of three adobe villages: the Spanish hamlet of Ranchos de Taos, the Spanish-Anglo village of Don Fernando de Taos and the Indian Pueblo of San Gerónimo de Taos.

The 12,000-foot-high sacred Taos Mountain and the surrounding landscape are dotted with gray-green *piñon*, juniper, golden aspen, ancient cottonwoods and apricot orchards. Buzzing with hummingbirds, they throw out a comforting mantle to cradle the trio of dusty towns, named "Taos," pronounced to rhyme with "house" and thought to be derived from an Indian word meaning "red willow."

An ancient land, the Taos Valley boasts a rich history of multicultures woven together like a brightly patterned Río Grande blanket. The first inhabitants were Anasazi Indians—the "Ancient Ones"—who settled here around 1000 A.D. Pit houses carved into the ground along *arroyos* and streams served as shelters for the tribes during the years preceding the building of pueblo structures. Over a hundred years before Christopher Columbus landed in the Americas, circa 1350 A.D., the Tiwa-speaking Indians constructed and inhabited the multistoried pueblo (Spanish for "village") they called "Tua-Tah" on the banks of the Río Pueblo.

In the year 1540, Spanish conquistador Don Hernando de Alvarado, scouting for famed explorer Francisco Vasquez de Coronado, discovered the straw-speckled terraced pueblos believing them to be one of the fabled "Golden Cities of Cibola." Declaring the region around the pueblo the province of the Spanish Crown, the conquistadores departed not to return until sixty years later in 1598 when Juan de Oñate, governor of *Nuevo Méjico*, dispatched as a missionary to the Taos region Fray Francisco de Zamora, who obtained an oath of allegiance from the pueblo. The Spanish settlers farmed the rich countryside creating a system of irrigation from *acequias,* or ditches. In 1680, under the crafty leadership of Popé, a medicine man from San Juan Pueblo, runners were sent across the *mesas* alerting the distant pueblos to their impending revolt. The Indians succeeded in driving the Spanish and their Franciscan missionaries out of northern New Mexico.

Sixteen years later, Don Diego de Vargas invaded the Taos Valley and restored twenty-three pueblos to the Spanish Empire. In the peaceful years that followed, the Spanish resettled around the Taos Pueblo, Taos Plaza and Ranchos de Taos. At the same time, expansive haciendas covering hundreds of acres carried on a thriving caravan business by way of the *Camino Real* to Chihuahua,

Mexico, a trip by ox carts, or *carretas*, and pack mules that took six months to complete. Trading, which had long taken place by Comanches, Utes and other tribes at Taos Pueblo, was carried on by French traders, led by the Mallette brothers. By the early 1800s, French and American trappers with their muzzle-loading rifles descended from the Sangre de Cristo Mountains. They were laden with skins and pelts, making Taos the center of the fur trade to St. Louis and a place to gamble, court women and drink hard whiskey, known as "Taos Lightning." Kit Carson, interpreter, trapper and scout, who arrived in 1826, was legendary among these mountain men.

In the 19th century, Taos was the scene of constant turmoil when New Mexico passed from Spanish rule to control by the new nation of Mexico and finally was acquired as a territory of the United States. These events, all happening within a span of thirty years, left *Taoseños* distrustful of outsiders, especially when their beloved land and precious water rights might be placed in jeopardy. With the Santa Fe Trail formally established in 1821, crossing into northeastern New Mexico at the "Cimarron Cutoff," Taos was bypassed and remained somewhat isolated from the outside world of commerce. During these years, Padre Antonio Martínez, the son of a hacienda landowner, who had studied for the priesthood in Durango, Mexico, accomplished a number of innovations for the Taos community. He established a coeducational school, the first in New Mexico, set up the second and most successful printing press west of the Mississippi and published the first newspaper, *El Crepúsculo de Libertad,* The

Dawn of Liberty, all while serving in the Mexican and New Mexican territorial legislative bodies.

In the 1890s the still-remote village of Taos, with just two thousand souls, was "discovered" as a place to paint by three accomplished artists who had studied in Paris: Joseph H. Sharp, Ernest L. Blumenschein and Bert G. Phillips. The serene adobe villages, the clear mountain light, the ever-changing landscape and the rich culture of the Indians offered the talented trio a vision of America, fresh and unspoiled, ready to be put on canvas. In 1914, joined by Oscar E. Berninghaus, E. Irving Couse and W. Herbert "Buck" Dunton, the six men formed the Taos Society of Artists. In the years that followed, the Society's work traveled the country, catching the fancy of the art-buying public.

The invasion of Taos by the colony of artists, along with latecomers like the Russian painters Leon Gaspard and Nicolai Fechin, was followed by avante-garde intellectuals, bohemians, performers and writers mesmerized by the Taos magic. It was the magnetic, wealthy and strong-willed Mabel Dodge Luhan who lured D. H. Lawrence, Georgia O'Keeffe and other "movers and shakers" to Los Gallos.

In the early decades of this century, Taos became the habitat of a host of colorful characters, like "Long" John Dunn, stagecoach owner and gambler; Arthur Manby, who by crooked and devious means acquired title to most of the Antonio Martínez Land Grant with tens of thousands of acres (his beheaded body was found in his hacienda in 1929); Doc Martin, the crusty physician, first in Taos, who treated gunshot wounds and delivered babies at his home, in what is now the historic Taos Inn.

In the late 1960s and early 1970s, swarms of young idealists descended on Taos with intentions to create their own utopia and make an impact on local politics. Blending into the diverse cultures they discovered here, the "hippies" perpetuated the cultural pluralism that makes for the "Old Taos Mystique." In the meantime, prolific writer Frank Waters, a Taos resident since the early 1930s, turned out book after book about the people of the Taos Valley. He wrote *The Man Who Killed The Deer* and *To Possess the Land*, both classics of their time and place. Other talented writers who made their mark in the Taos Valley were Blanche Chloe Grant, "The Taos Historian," Claire Morrill, author of *A Taos Mosaic,* and John Nichols, who penned *The Milagro Beanfield War*, among dozens of others.

Today, the verdant valley of the Pueblo Indians, the Spanish conquistadores and cara-

van traders, the French and American trappers and trailblazers, the magical mission churches and mysterious *moradas* awaits the visitor. Here one can explore the skylit studios where the Anglo artists worked at their easels. Here one can stroll the tree-shaded plaza where "Old Glory" flies both day and night, as well as the serene *placitas* lined with hollyhocks and silvery gray Russian olive trees where blue, black and white magpies mingle. Here, one can visit the peach, pink and ochre-colored *casas* and *casitas* where Taos writers, weavers, potters and poets reside.

Add to these treasures hiking the vast Carson National Forest, with its countless trails and rushing rock-strewn streams, high-country skiing in the breathtaking Taos Ski Valley on world-class slopes amid snow-covered pines and corkbark trees, whitewater rafting through the surging Río Grande Gorge—all enlivened by ethnic festivals, a hot-air balloon rally and mouth-watering Southwestern cuisine served in romantic candlelit *cantinas*. Taken together, they create the marvelous mosaic that encompasses the landmarks and legends of Taos.

High Road to Taos
Shepherds, Master Weavers, Santuarios and Miracles

There are two routes one can take to Taos from Santa Fe and the south. One is New Mexico 68 that swiftly follows the curves and canyons along the jade-green, swirling Río Grande. The other, New Mexico 76 to 518, affectionately called the "high road" or the "back way," takes over an hour longer but rewards the scenery-seeker with stops at sleepy Spanish villages, visits to ancient adobe *santuarios* and opportunities to watch master weavers working at their looms. All this, topped off by the majestic vista of the Sangre de Cristo (blood of Christ) Mountains.

If one travels east, then north, the first destination on the itinerary is the chamisa-strewn Chimayó Valley which was occupied by the Anasazi, "The Ancient Ones," centuries before the arrival of Coronado, who brought sheep into New Mexico in 1540. Here, along the Santa Cruz River, dozes the sleepy Spanish village of Cañada de Chimayó, as it was called in the early records. Chimayó lies just fifteen miles from San Gabriel, now in ruins beside the Río Grande, the old capital of New Mexico established by Juan de Oñate in 1598. Chimayó has been a center of the Spanish weaving tradition for more than 250 years. For eight generations, ever since Gabriel Ortega, in the early 1700s, first built his two-harness, horizontal treadle loom and began weaving, the Ortega family has turned out the softly colored Chimayó blankets, rugs, coats, vests, purses and cushions, all in 100% wool. Today, with David Ortega now retired, his two sons, Andrew and Robert, carry on the time-honored tradition that draws travelers from afar.

Strolling through the town's Spanish Colonial *Plaza del Cerro*, one can admire a national treasure built between 1680 and 1692. It is one of the most intact examples of a fortified complex in the Southwest. The old adobes still form the square of the fort with an old *torreón*, or guard tower, still standing outside the plaza. Just a short walk up the road stands the *Santuario de Chimayó*. This little church, entered through an old oaken gate and a walled garden with stout arbor vitae shrubs standing guard, is known for its remarkable healing powers, bringing over 300,000 pilgrims every year to Chimayó.

A simple shepherd, Don Bernardo Abeyta, crippled with arthritis, was cured by bathing his body in the muddy soil here. In a truly mystical experience, Abeyta saw a vision of the crucified Christ.

Abeyta, along with fellow citizens of El Potrero, built this wonderful example of Spanish Colonial architecture in 1816. Laying out the floor of the side chapel, they decided to leave a small opening so worshipers and pilgrims, seeking healing and tranquility, might continue the tradition of touching the sacred earth and taking small amounts of the holy dirt back to their homes. As testimony to the shrine's miraculous healing powers, rows of crutches, braces, pictures of people restored to health and tokens of appreciation from the "cures of the faithful" hang from the ceiling of the candle-lit chapel. In the interior of the twin-belfried *santuario* honoring *Nuestro Señor de Esquipulas*, one finds magnificent altar screens containing a series of sacred paintings of saints. The largest painting is behind the main altar, created by Molleno, also known by the nickname of "The Chile Painter."

Here in Chimayó, parishioners also claim that the Christ Child, *El Santo Niño de Atocha*, the lost Holy Child, walks the lanes and orchards by night, healing and comforting sick children and bringing baskets of food to prisoners in jail. Gourds of water hang from his staff. Not far from the *santuario* huddles the *Santo Niño* chapel built in 1857 by Blas Seberiano Medina. A private chapel, it is dedicated to the *Santo Niño* whose statue was brought to Chimayó from Fresnio, Mexico. Legend has it that the statue becomes animated at night and performs miracles and good deeds for the faithful. The story of *El Santo Niño* originated in Spain during medieval times when Moors held large areas of the land and battles with Christians were commonplace. Following one particular battle, the victorious Moors held hundreds of Christians captive, forbidding villagers to bring them aid. Then one night a child appeared carrying a basket filled with food and gourds containing cool water. The Moors per-

mitted the little one to visit and bring nourishment to the prisoners. The Christians of that time concluded that the Child Jesus, disguised as a pilgrim, had come to the prisoners' rescue.

Before leaving Chimayó, the itinerant gourmet should not miss a stop at the Rancho de Chimayó, basking in the shade of an ancient catalpa tree, its *portals* festooned with red chile *ristras*. Situated in the ancestral home of Hermenegildo and Trinidad Jaramillo, the restaurant is known throughout the region for its unique New Mexican cuisine prepared with locally grown products from recipes that have been in the family for eight generations.

A northerly route up amid spectacular badlands through a patchwork quilt of farms, fruit orchards and chile fields leads to the rustic hamlet of Truchas, "The Trout," 8,000 feet high, hugging a hogback overlooking the Truchas Peaks. Ice-age glaciers carved these beautiful alpine mountains, among the highest in the New Mexico Rockies, rising to 13,101 feet. Not much has changed here since it was established in the mid-18th century as "Our Lady of the Rosary of the Trout." The village's thick-adobe-walled houses, ramshackle stores and surrounding fields served as the location for the film classic, *The Milagro Beanfield War*, based on the John

Nichols novel and directed by Robert Redford. As beans are known not to thrive at this altitude, the production staff had to import the plants from a lower area farm and place them in the Truchas fields.

The Cordova family of master hand weavers makes its home here, where visitors are welcome to browse through their busy workshop. Five looms turn out multicolored rugs and thick wool blankets that please the eye.

Continuing north, the next destination is Las Trampas, "The Traps," settled in 1751 by twelve families from Santa Fe, led by Juan de Arguello, who received a land grant from Governor Tomas Velez Cachupin. The crown jewel of this diminutive town is the classic church, La Iglesia de San José de Gracia, one of the most imposing examples of Spanish Colonial architecture. It boasts four-foot-thick adobe walls that rise to a height of thirty feet. Constructed in 1760, "The Church of the Twelve Apostles" was so named because the twelve men who had settled there did the building. The spacious interior, with massive *vigas* in the ceiling, contains precious treasures of

ecclesiastical art, exquisite hand-carved *bultos* and brilliantly painted *retablos*.

In 1970, the church was listed on the National Register of Historic Places as a means of protecting it from a planned highway that would have sliced the town in two. Thankfully, the now completely restored sanctuary, with its gentler-toned *gracia* bell in one belfry ringing for mass and its stronger-toned *refugio* bell in the other, which mourns the deaths of adults, invites visitors to venture inside for a quiet prayer or a peaceful moment of reflection.

Next, the route north takes one through Peñasco, past the ancient Picuris Pueblo, and through the tiny hamlet of Vadito. It skirts the ski valley of Sipapu before passing through the picturesque village of Talpa, with its ancient *torreón*, or fortified circular tower. One finally arrives at the three historic towns that spill across the Taos Valley like amber jewels on green velvet: Ranchos de Taos, Don Fernando de Taos and the Pueblo of San Gerónimo de Taos. Each one basks in bright sunshine under an azure sky; each one winks a warm welcome. With the high road now traversed, the landmarks and legends of Taos await exploration, enlightenment and enjoyment. *¡Bienvenidos!*

It happened in Italy at the turn of the 13th century. A dashing young nobleman, about to join the Crusade to regain the Holy Land from the Saracens, became gravely ill and was unable to take the journey. While he was recovering, a vision appeared to him saying: "Go, Francis, build up my house for it is nearly falling into ruin." Accepting the challenge, the man who would eventually be canonized St. Francis of Assisi (1181-1226 A.D.), proceeded to rebuild many of the ancient churches of Europe, stone by stone, establishing religious reform and performing numerous miracles.

It was the humble friar's example that in 1979 inspired the congregation of San Francisco de Asís Church at Ranchos de Taos to rebuild their age-old sanctuary, the façade of which was cracking and crumbling before their very eyes. A decade before, the adobe walls had been "protected" with modern wire and cement. This proved to be a serious mistake as rainwater had entered through the cracks in the cement surface, moistening and eventually destroying the adobe bricks inside. All twelve hundred families in the close-knit Ranchos parish pitched in for the reconstruction.

First, the men mixed the adobe just as it was done almost 200 years ago, by hand or shovel. Traditionally, Hispanic and Indian men mixed the mud with binders, usually straw, and a little sand. Next, they pressed this mixture into molds to form the bricks. Then the still-wet shapes were quickly removed and put on the ground to dry. When the thousands upon thousands of adobe bricks were dried out by the intense New Mexico sunlight, it was time to begin the rebuilding. Once the concrete skin of the church's exterior was pulled off with crowbars, axes and jackhammers, the water-soaked buttresses had to be removed brick by brick and rebuilt with fresh new adobe blocks on new foundations. When the church walls had been reconstructed, the exposed adobe bricks were covered with two layers of a mud and straw mixture prepared by the parish women, called *enjarradoras,* or plasterers, who wear mud-splattered bandanas, a custom for countless generations.

Once the exterior walls had been stroked by many hands dipped into soft mud, the interior walls were then finished over with a mixture of glossy clay. While still damp the last layer was smoothed on by the hands of the Ranchos women. The finish slip, or coat, was pure earth, finely screened, mixed to a soupy consistency and applied with sheepskin, brush, sponge or hand. The most commonly used color, *tierra blanca*, is a whitewash or jaspe of native micaceous gypsum, which is baked, pulverized and mixed with water and flour for use on the interior walls.

Today, thanks to the diligent work done by the men and women of the Ranchos parish, San Francisco de Asís ranks as one of the most beautiful edifices in New Mexico. What's more, the 120-foot-long landmark, with its powerful but softly contoured buttresses that support adobe walls six feet thick at the base and grow progressively thinner to four feet as they reach its great height, is probably the most painted, sketched and photographed religious structure in the United States. What captivates the visitor to Ranchos de Taos are the changing shadows cast by the sun as it moves across the brilliant blue sky making the mission church all the more intriguing and inspiring.

If the church on the bumpy plaza closely resembles a little fortress, especially from the rear of the building that faces the road to Santa Fe, there are good reasons. The Pueblo Indians and the Spanish settlers who lived in Ranchos, originally called *Las Trampas* when it was first founded in 1725, faced a common enemy: bands of Apaches, Comanches and Utes who swooped down into the valley for food, livestock and slaves. As a result, the flanking bell towers, one slightly taller than the other, in true Taos lack of precision, were built to face east, the rising sun and the Sangre de Cristo Mountains from which the rampaging hordes came. Originally, the church was without windows in its thick ramparts so as to provide a safe haven for the parishioners when under attack. Later, in the 19th century, when peace finally came to Ranchos de Taos, two Palladian-influenced

arched windows were placed in the walls flooding the dark church with warm sunlight.

Built circa 1815, under the direction of the Franciscan Friar, Jose Benito Pereyro, in the usual cruciform shape with stout *vigas* in the ceiling, the church contains marvelous screens behind the main and side altars. One contains a brightly colored *bulto* of St. Francis, a masterpiece of Spanish Colonial art. The *retablos* and *bultos* on the northeast screen were created by Molleno, an early 19th century *santero*.

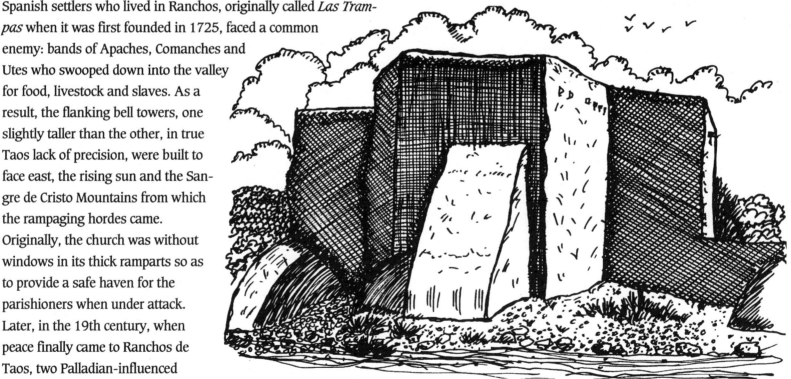

In the church rectory across the plaza, visitors can marvel at the mystery painting, *The Shadow of the Cross*, completed by Henri Ault in 1896. The picture is most extraordinary in that while seen in daylight, it portrays Christ standing on the shore of Lake Galilee. With the lights turned off for ten minutes and in complete darkness, the portrait gradually becomes luminescent, outlining the glowing white figure while clouds over the left shoulder of Jesus form into a shadow of a cross. Because he created the painting several years before the discovery of radium, Ault, the artist, quite believably disclaimed any knowledge of the reason for the miraculous change. Displayed at the St. Louis World's Fair in 1904, then taken to London and on tours of the continent, the painting was finally presented to the Ranchos church in 1948 along with other historic and valuable works of art. In the flower-filled front courtyard many Ranchos parishioners are buried. The main church door is a folk-style adaptation of the Gothic Revival design. Present-day parishioners attend church as their ancestors did for over a century before them, praying in the sanctuary built of the soil. Many have the same names that appeared on the roll of Oñate's original group of 1598. October 4th, the feast of their patron saint, Francis of Assisi, remains a day dear to the hearts of the Ranchos people. It is a time to rekindle their faith in God and devotion to the simple adobe church they shaped with their own bare hands. Visitors who come from far and wide to see the sanctuary tell the parishioners how beautiful it looks. And in their own humble way, like Francis, the Patron Saint of Ecology, an angel in human flesh whom the birds and animals delighted in being near, they accept the compliment with modest appreciation.

BILL HEMP

Martínez Hacienda

Caravans of Carretas on the Camino Real

This classical fortress-style compound sitting defiantly on the banks of the Río Pueblo, two miles southeast of Taos Plaza on Ranchitos Road, is one of the few remaining haciendas in New Mexico open to the public. Inside the massive adobe walls one is offered a glimpse of Spanish Colonial life as it was experienced almost 200 years ago. In 1804, Don Antonio Severino Martín (later changed to Martínez) purchased the land by the river from two Indians and moved his family from Abiquiu into a small dwelling consisting of four rooms that existed at that time. As his family grew, Martínez began expanding the complex, until by the time of his death in 1827, the structure contained twenty-one rooms with the main living quarters surrounding a large *placita* with a well to the east and the servants' quarters, *granero*, tack room and blacksmith shop facing a smaller courtyard to the west.

Today, a visit to the fully restored hacienda vividly brings to life the daily routines and rich traditions of the Spanish settlers. Its exterior and interior walls are finished with mud plaster, while the pearl-white interior walls are finished in *tierra blanca*, a rare white micaceous soil found near Taos. Fourteen of the rooms have floors made of mud. The *sala,* with its split cedar ceiling, served as a formal parlor for relatives and visitors. It contained the Martínez family's prized possessions, such as large, intricately carved wooden chests. Because of the family's importance in the community, Don Severino had a *gran sala* constructed with a hand-adzed floor and a rugged surface for political meetings and gay fandangos. The spacious room features two fireplaces in opposite corners and two hanging wooden candleholders that are fine examples of the earliest imported light fixtures. The Spanish brought candles and the knowledge of candlemaking back in the 16th century, but materials were rare and candles were used mostly in churches and the homes of the wealthy.

From the *gran sala* one steps into *la despensa,* which functioned as a pantry and cool room for storing meats, fruits and vegetables. Herbs and dried game were hung from poles attached to the split aspen ceiling. Squash, apples, potatoes and other garden produce were covered with layers of straw and stored inside large adobe bins placed on the floor to preserve them through the bitter cold Taos winters. *La cocina*, equipped with a shepherd's hearth, allowed for an extensive cooking area with a large bell-shaped flue for drawing out smoke and with space above for sleeping and storage. It was obviously a busy place, feeding family and servants three meals a day. In the trade room, one sees the items Don Severino took to Mexico by caravan and would barter and trade: animal skins, grain, jerked meat, wool and *piñón* nuts. In the early 19th century the only supplies to Taos came by ox cart and pack mule from the annual trade fair in Chihuahua, Mexico.

In early times, trade roads radiated like the spokes of a wheel from Mexico City. The longest ran northward about 1200 miles to the frontier province of New Mexico. The northern road was known as *el camino de tierra adentro*, or "the road from the interior." This path extended from Mexico City, through Durango, Chihuahua, El Paso del Norte, and Santa Fe and finally to Taos. From Mexico came sugar, chocolate, tools made of iron, shoes, writing paper, ink and religious objects. The Taos Trade Fair was traditionally held around harvest time in early October and well before the annual caravan departed for Chihuahua. New Mexican merchants embarking for this destination formed their own protective caravans, *conductas*, to transport their products, which included buffalo robes, tanned deer hides, elk, antelope, beaver and woolen stockings.

Rising from modest beginnings to a position of commercial and political prominence, Don Severino built a new way of life at the hacienda, amassing caravans of *carretas* and pack mules necessary for the Chihuahua trade on the *Camino Real*, the royal highway. He also held the office of *alcalde*, mayor of Taos, for a number of years. His eldest son, Antonio José, entered the priesthood in Durango, Mexico, and went on to exert tremendous influence as spiritual and social leader of the northern Río Grande area. Commerce in the caravan trade was carried on by Martínez's youngest son, Don Juan Pascual, who became the eventual owner of the sprawling hacienda.

With no exterior windows in its thick walls, the self-contained compound served as home and refuge for the Martínez family against fearful raids by Apache and Comanche Indians. In addition to the unbroken circuit of exterior walls, the adobe parapet was originally constructed high enough to protect the guards who, during surprise attacks, defended the rooftops. Loopholes, or *troneras*, were cut through the upper walls. Access by ladder to the roof was gained through a hatchway from the patio *portal*. Livestock were driven through the *zaguánes*, or covered passageways with heavy

the exhibit room, which harbors a striking assemblage of rare *santos*. *Bultos* are three-dimensional carvings of saints and holy persons. *Retablos* are pictures of saints painted on flat wooden tablets for hanging on a wall. *Cristos* are large effigies of Christ on the cross that are still used by the brotherhood of *Penitentes* and carried in processions during Holy Week in Lent.

In 1972, in conjunction with its Spanish Culture Program, the Kit Carson Foundation acquired La Hacienda de Don Antonio Severino Martinez, which had fallen into ruin, and three and one-half acres of the original land grant. Now completely restored, the walled compound has been designated as a Registered National Historic Building by the National Park Service.

protective gates called *puertones*, and into the peaceful *placitas* until the raid was over. Today, in front of the hacienda's fortlike façade one can inspect a replica of an 18th century ox cart from the bygone days of caravans of *carretas* and observe that each wheel was cut from one piece of wood and attached to a wooden axle with pegs. Just a stone's throw away stand two beehive-shaped ovens, or *hornos*, built by artisan Carmen Velarde. A Moor-influenced Spanish introduction brought by the settlers who came to the Taos valley in 1750, the *horno* was made of adobe and used primarily for baking bread. A fire is first made in the oven and allowed to burn down to glowing coals. After the ashes are removed, the dough is placed inside the hot chamber and the doorway closed with a flat stone. A delicate wheaten loaf is the happy result! The *horno* is still in common use throughout the Indian pueblos and in some rural Hispanic villages.

Walking past the compound's stone-ringed water well, strategically located inside the large *placita* where it served the family when confined during enemy assaults, the visitor finally arrives at

BILL HEMP

Don Fernando de Taos Plaza
Gunfights, Fiestas and a Fought-Over Flagpole

Since the 1790s, it has been the site of gun brawls, fiery speeches, military encampments, riotous mobs and a series of disastrous fires. Today, the plaza serves as the tree-shaded hub of Taos, complete with a historic flagpole. There is also a massive cross created by sculptor Ted Egri in memory of the *Taoseños* who died in the Bataan Death March during World War II, a gazebo bandstand for fiesta frolics and four sides of galleries, shops and restaurants catering to visitors arriving from places like Peoria, Peking and Paris.

In pioneer days, the Taos Plaza was surrounded by homes belonging to early Spanish settlers. But by 1903 most of these had gone with the wind or been converted into commercial enterprises. Juan Santistevan, whom most townspeople called "the richest man in Taos," owned most of the north side of the plaza. The leading business establishments in the early years of this century included Gerson Gusdorf's General Merchandise Store, billed as "the largest mercantile enterprise away from the railroad," the Miles Boyer Grocery, Bill Hinde's Blacksmith Shop, the DesGeorges Dance Hall and Harry Tarleton's Garage. In those bygone days, *Taoseño* children could go down to the town's candy store and pick up four licorice sticks that cost them just one penny!

Nowadays, *Taoseños* and tourists alike can enjoy window-shopping in the plaza beneath the welcoming shade of the *portals*, where shiny red chile *ristras* hang from stout pine *vigas* pro-truding from mud-brown adobe walls. Even on the hottest days in summer one can browse in comfort on all sides of the plaza, where galleries and gift shops stand cheek by jowl, offering everything from landscape paintings and intricate Navajo rugs to turquoise jewelry and western attire, consisting of boots, buckles, bolos, concho belts and hatbands.

During the annual Fiesta de Santiago y Santa Ana, historic Taos Plaza becomes the town's central focus with residents celebrating the proud heritage they have shared since the community was first colonized by the Spanish in the 1790s. The name *Don Fernando* dates to Captain Don Fernando de Chavez, a prominent land grant owner in the Taos area in 1680. The Don Fernando de Taos Grant was given to sixty-three Spanish families on May 1, 1796. The name Taos is believed to be an adaptation of the Tiwa Indian word, "towih," meaning "red willow." It was first recorded in history by Juan Belarde, Secretary to the Governor, Juan de Oñate, in 1598.

At fiesta time, a carnival atmosphere prevails with parades of floats, open "low rider" convertibles, often of 1950s vintage, carrying the lovely fiesta queen and her comely court. Sleek black stallions pull old-fashioned buggies, and flat-bed trucks are festooned with colorful ribbons. The center of attraction for children is *El Tio Vivo*, "the Lively Uncle," an old-fashioned wooden carousel, one of the oldest in existence at an estimated

167 years. When Taos artists were asked to paint the carousel's 12 horses, they responded with artistic abandon, converting the merry-go-round into a colorful, movable feast for the eyes. Traditionally, *El Tio Vivo* remains a headline attraction at the fiesta, carrying 400 delighted passengers an hour, transporting young riders into a fantasy land of excitement and adventure. In 1995, the carousel makes its 57th annual appearance at the fiesta.

Around the plaza colorful food kiosks spill over with a cornucopia of Southwestern delicacies: fiery-hot Indian tacos, tamales, *sopaipillas* and bulging burritos covered with a heaping topping of red or green chile. All kinds of music—country, rock 'n' roll, mariachi and the traditional Spanish—emanate from the gazebo, donated by Mabel Dodge Luhan, for the entertainment of all.

La Fonda de Taos, the hotel built in 1937 by John and James Karavas on the south side of the plaza, has been a magnet over the years, attracting authors, actors, playwrights and painters to its cluttered but intriguing interior lobby. Gary Cooper, Tennessee Williams and Robert Oppenheimer, father of the atomic bomb, all stayed in the storied establishment. Fox star, Tyrone Power, and his first wife, Annabella, honeymooned here. Probably the biggest drawing card to the hotel is a collection of erotic paintings created by D. H. Lawrence, the British author, who spent several years on and off in Taos. The controversial canvases were purchased by La Fonda owner Saki Karavas, an American-born Greek. He is also the proud owner of a private edition of *Lady Chatterly's Lover*, No. 990, autographed by the writer.

The old courthouse on the north side of the plaza, with cell blocks on the lower level, is renowned for the Taos murals that decorate the main courtroom on the second floor. Emil Bisttram, who studied with Diego Rivera in Mexico, enlisted Taos artists Victor Higgins and Bert Phillips, together with Ward Lockwood, to paint the ten meaningful frescos, each one financed by a 1934 WPA Arts Project. Used as the Taos courthouse until 1969, the territorial-style structure served as one locale for the film *Easy Rider*, starring Dennis Hopper, Peter Fonda and Jack Nicholson. Opened in 1970 as the Taos Art Center, the jail, along with the solitary confinement cell, now displays the work of local artists such as Miguel Martínez, Evalena and JD Challenger.

During the 1930s Oscar Berninghaus drew a cartoon of Taos Plaza showing the famous residents congregating outside the old Don Fernando Hotel. The cast of colorful characters included Mabel Dodge Luhan, Dorothy Brett, Jerry Mirabal, the Indian who met and entertained all tourists, Gerson Gusdorf, who built the hotel, "Long" John Dunn and Leon Gaspard with his sketchpad. Helen Blumenschein's coupe is seen making a swift turn in front of doughBelly Price's real estate office, which he called "the clip joint." Next to the hotel was the old movie theater managed by Jack Brandenburg, with the popular popcorn concession run by his wife, Dorothy. Funk's 5- and 10-cent store is not seen in the picture but drew droves of customers back in those depression days. A favorite eatery then was La Cocina, whose walls were covered with colorful murals featuring the celebrated citizens of Taos.

During the Civil War, Taos became a hotbed of Confederate sympathy. The South's strategy involved controlling the gold and silver mines of the Southwest in order to support military operations in the East. Kit Carson, in company with Smith Simpson, Cerain St. Vrain and Tom Boggs, fearing that the restless Confederate troops then stationed in Taos might take over the town, dispatched a man to the mountains to cut down a tall cottonwood tree. They then nailed the Stars and Stripes to the stripped bark and raised the pole over the plaza. Carson and his cohorts stood guard on the rooftops surrounding the square with rifles ready, daring any comer to rip down the Star Spangled Banner. Not a soul stepped forward. After Union troops from Colorado defeated a Confederate troop in the bloody battle at Glorieta Pass on March 28, 1862, the Confederacy's foothold in New Mexico faded into oblivion.

Now, at the west end of the plaza high above a flagstone platform and shaded by a lofty cottonwood, the American flag flutters in sunshine by day and moonlight by night. Authorized by an act of the United States Congress in recognition of the Union Army's heroic stand at Glorieta, the Town of Taos is one of just five places in America permitted this great honor.

BILL HEMP

Kit Carson Home and Museum

Trapper, Trail Blazer, Scout and Soldier

In 1826, Christopher "Kit" Carson, a young boy of seventeen caught by the "fever of the frontier," ran away from his apprenticeship with a Missouri saddlemaker and joined a wagon train heading for Santa Fe, New Mexico. Captivated by the wild beauty of Taos, Carson stayed on in the valley first as a cook, then as an interpreter, and finally achieved the status of a trapper. At that time, blessed by an abundance of beaver in the streams fed by the Sangre de Cristo Mountains, Taos was the center of the fur trade. In the adventure-filled years that followed, Kit hunted buffalo, led the way for John C. Fremont, "the pathfinder," and guided General Stephen Kearny around the West.

Married first to an Arapahoe Indian woman named Wah-Nibe, then after her death to a Jicarilla Apache, "Making-Out-Road," whom he divorced, Carson bought this twelve-room adobe house in 1843 as a wedding present for his new bride, 14-year-old Josepha Jaramillo, the darkly beautiful daughter of an influential Taos family. Built in 1825, the one-story house was cooled in summers and warmed in winters by 30-inch-thick walls and fat ceiling beams or *vigas*. It contained stables and corrals around a central patio and well. Seen on a visit today behind its storefront façade are eight information-filled rooms depicting the life and times of the legendary mountain man and Union Army officer.

The home and museum contain a treasury of original expedition maps, personal possessions, uniforms, frocks, artifacts and furnishings that dramatically bring to life the artists, ranchers, trappers and adventure-loving individualists, the brave and hardy souls who made Taos the crossroads of the Southwest during the rambunctious 19th century.

In the museum's first chamber, called the Carson Interpretive Room, a visitor can trace the chronology of the scout's event-filled career, touch the cradle in which Kit and his brothers and sister were rocked back in Kentucky, where he was born December 24, 1809, the same year Abraham Lincoln was birthed in a log cabin just 50 miles away. Along with a number of photographs of Kit, with or without his mustache, one can admire the Spencer Repeating Carbine which he used during the Civil War and the Indian Campaign. Beside it hangs the buckskin rifle boot made by a Taos Indian friend that snugly fits the Spencer. In an adjacent exhibit case hangs his handsome pipe and tobacco pouch, a beaded work of Indian art that provides a touch of nostalgia for days in the wilderness of the vast Southwest.

Noteworthy are the Indian, Taos and Carson Rooms that capture the feel of "the Old West" at its best. In the Indian Room, one can spend minutes at a time looking over each one of the interesting artifacts made and used by the original inhabitants of the Taos Valley. Carson served as an Indian Agent from 1854 to 1861 for the Taos Pueblo, Jicarilla Apache, Muhuache and Ute Tribes for several years, using his home for conducting this business. The

Taos Room exhibits articles used by friends of the Carsons including the fancy wedding dresses, bustled evening gowns, dainty shoes and delicate shawls the *Taoseña* ladies wore during those frontier days and nights. A featured attraction in this room is the mahogany-brown, hand-tooled leather western saddle once owned by the artist W. Herbert "Buck" Dunton, noted for his portrayals in oils of cowboys, cowgirls and bronco-busters.

The three rooms in the front of the house, the Carson Living Room, the bedroom and the kitchen with its *fogón de campana,* a bell-shaped fireplace that allowed a cook to work at both open sides, are furnished today with antiques and artifacts as they might have looked when the Carson family of eight children along with several members of the Jaramillo and Bent families, as well as the Indian children Kit and Josepha had adopted, lived there. In the cozy parlor, the Carsons entertained U.S. Army officers, government officials, scouts and anyone else who knocked on the door. Of special interest are the desk and game table used religiously by Kit and the painting of Carson by Blanche Chloe Grant, the Taos artist and historian, which dominates the corner fireplace.

Well over a century after his death, the debate over Kit Carson continues unabated. Was he a great hero or a blood-thirsty villain? The facts or fiction presented by his supporters and detractors provide a plethora of stories about one of the most famous 19th century men to roam the West. During the Civil War, the 5'8" barrel-chested Carson, who possessed piercing blue-gray eyes and a drooping reddish mustache, joined the Union Army "Blue Coats" against the Confederate "Gray Coats." He was known by the Navajo Indians as

"the Rope Thrower." They respected him as a fighter but harbored intense hatred for his ragtag horde of soldiers.

In January of 1864, under strict orders from Brigadier General James H. Carleton, who had nothing but scorn for the Indians, Carson unleashed a scorched-earth program in Arizona's Canyon de Chelly, a Navajo stronghold cutting westward for 30 miles from the Chuska Mountains. Here in the red-rocked and walled valleys, the Indians lived in their mound-shaped hogans and raised corn, goats and sheep. Still, their real pride lay in their peach orchards, carefully cultivated from early Spanish days. Before returning to headquarters at Fort Canby, Carson directed the destruction of all the properties within the canyon, spoiling wells and destroying over two million pounds of Navajo grain. After surrendering, some 8,000 Navajos were clothed and fed by Carson but then were forced to make the journey from the canyon in Arizona across New Mexico to Bosque Redondo, east of Albuquerque. The tragic 250-mile march that

took a tremendous toll in Indian lives is remembered today as the "Long Walk." In the summer of 1864, months after Kit had been relieved as field commander, troops under Captain John Thompson cut down nearly 5,000 of the Navajos' beloved peach trees.

In an interview recorded by Brigadier General James F. Rustling at Fort Garland, Colorado, in 1866, Kit Carson is quoted while discussing his feelings about Native Americans: "I tell ye what: I don't like a hostile Red Skin any better than you do. And when they're hostile, I've fit 'em—fout 'em—as hard as any a man. But I never yit drew a bead on a squaw or papoose, and I loathe and hate the man who would. T'aint natural for brave men to kill women and little children, and no one but a coward or a dog would do it."

Although unable to read or write, Carson had a rare talent for language. He spoke Spanish as well as, if not better than, English, and was able to communicate in French, Navajo, Apache, Comanche, Cheyenne, Arapahoe, Crow, Blackfoot, Shoshone, Paiute and Ute, as well as the universal sign language. Not until Kit became an Indian Agent did he learn to write his name, probably by copying his signature as originally written by someone else.

In his later years, after serving as Fremont's guide through the Rockies to Oregon and California on three exploring expeditions, the stocky Carson, who looked quite regal when mounted upon his

(Drawing of Kit Carson after a photograph courtesy of The Kit Carson Museum.)

favorite horse, Apache, thought nothing of a horseback ride of 75 or 100 miles a day. Carson even tried his hand at ranching from 1847 to 1853, during which time he drove 6,500 sheep from New Mexico to California through hostile Indian territory, turning a profit of $35,000.

In early 1868, Carson was appointed Superintendent of Indian Affairs for the Colorado Territory, where he negotiated the treaty for the Ute Indians. On May 23, "Dear Old Kit" died of an aneurysm exactly one month after his wife, Josepha, whom he called Chipita, died of complications resulting from childbirth. Thus passed away one of the truly remarkable figures in the drama that unfolded in the West—a man who lived life to the fullest and saw more than most would even dare dream. Married three times and buried three times, Kit Carson is remembered as a soft-spoken man of honor who "never cussed more'n was necessary." First buried at Fort Lyons, then moved to Boggsville, Colorado where his children lived, the couple's remains were later transferred to Taos, as they had wished, to a plot in what is today known as the Kit Carson Cemetery. The Carson house was sold in 1869. Between that year and 1910, the property changed hands six times before being purchased by Bent Lodge No. 43. Since 1952 the adobe structure has been operated by the Kit Carson Memorial Foundations as a historic house and museum. Kit and Chipita would be content.

Studios of Joseph H. Sharp and E.I. Couse

Two American Painters Bid Paris Adieu for Taos

Entering through a blue gate from Kit Carson Road, the visitor is welcomed by an *oratorio* built of adobe by Juan de Luna about 1835, dedicated to San Antonio de Padua and shaded by a towering spruce. This was the original studio of the "Patriarch Painter," Joseph Henry Sharp, one of the first Anglo artists to visit the Taos Valley. It was he who announced to fellow students back in Paris that the area was a perfect place to paint. Sharp, who also studied in Antwerp and Munich, purchased property to the west for his house, acquired the chapel in 1909 and used it as his "Copper Bell Studio," named for the rusty old Spanish bell in the cupola, dated 1868, which he purchased at the Taos Pueblo.

Sharp made some modifications to the *oratorio*, installing a large studio window to bring in north light, a fireplace and a wooden floor. He later put in a spacious storage vault, using a door obtained from a failed Taos bank, in which were safeguarded his precious canvases. Beginning in 1902, Sharp, deaf from birth, who learned to read lips and never went anywhere without a pencil and a pad of paper, usually stayed and painted several months of the year in Taos. However, feeling that their culture would soon fade away, he was determined to first paint the Plains Indians in Montana. He worked there in the "Prairie Dog," a cattle herder's commissary wagon converted into his studio-on-wheels. This was just twenty-five years after General George Armstrong Custer and the Seventh Cavalry were defeated by Sitting Bull and Crazy Horse in 1876 at the Battle of Little Bighorn that turned the tide of history.

Enjoying great success with his portraits of Indians, Sharp was particularly admired for his anthropological accuracy and depiction of the physical characteristics of the various tribes as well as for his documentation of costumes, accouterments and rituals of Indian life on the Plains and in Taos. This is certainly evident in such canvases as *The Bow and Arrow Maker*, *Chant to the Warbonnet* and *Meditation of a Young Medicine Man*, who is seen in a dark corner lighted by a glowing fire in the *kiva* fireplace. When Phoebe Apperson Hearst, mother of William Randolph Hearst, the publisher, purchased eighty of his paintings for the University of California in 1902, a jubilant Sharp was able to give up teaching art in Cincinnati and take up a career of landscape and portrait painting in the West.

It is said that while in Montana, Sharp completed paintings of over two hundred Indian survivors of the Battle of Little Bighorn, including his portrait of the Crow Indian named "Curley," Custer's famous scout and the only one to escape the bloody conflict alive. He also painted "White Swan," Reno's scout in the battle, who was picked up on the field two days later, struck deaf and dumb by the blow of a war club on his forehead. Settling in Taos permanently in 1912, the bearded artist built a new studio behind his house in 1915, where he was "busy every minute, 24 hours a day," painting his beloved Indians until just before his death in 1953. It is now the workspace of *bulto* and *retablo* artist Victor Goler.

Opening a rustic wooden door carved with the words "Couse Studio," one enters the compound of Eanger Irving Couse. He was born in Saginaw, Michigan, in 1866 and studied at the National Academy of Design in New York and the Académie Julian in Paris. Here sprawls an L-shaped, old-fashioned house that hugs a hilltop overlooking a verdant pasture where Arabian horses graze and offers a splendid view of the snow-capped Truchas Peaks to the south.

In 1902, when Couse arrived in Taos, he discovered just about everything he had hoped for in the way of artistic inspiration. He found in Native American culture an inner spirituality, which he captured through his handsome figures and quiet scenes. What's more, he admired the Pueblo Indians as artists and craftsmen, and their artifacts played an important part in his compositions. Completely fulfilled by the Taos tableau, Couse was to spend the rest of his life painting Native Americans.

Walking past a terraced garden filled with poppies planted by Couse's wife, Virginia, then over a boardwalk beneath a *portal* to a bronze plaque commemorating the Italian artist Titian, one enters the Couse living room. It is furnished with 18th century Spanish pieces and an elegant wooden bench designed by the artist. From this room one enters the spacious studio Couse created by raising a high window above the roof, facing true north, with an unusual shingling of glass panes. Today, the Couse studio serves as a time warp. Here stands his easel, a lone sentinel to a great talent, and a brass-hinged tabaret with three drawers filled with hundreds of his paintbrushes. An adobe fireplace in the corner recreates the effect of a pueblo interior, which Couse so often included in his paintings. On a shelf above sits his colorful collection of antique Indian pottery.

While the rotund Couse was essentially a studio painter, he did enjoy putting on his ever-present green sweater, which earned him the Indian nickname Green Mountain, and going down to the

Río Grande to do *plein air* studies. He liked to paint the Indians in a landscape, as this was their natural environment. Jerry Mirabel, Elk-Foot, of Taos Pueblo, who started posing for Couse in 1907, was one of Couse's favorite models because of his aristocratic good looks and natural grace. The painting *Elk-Foot of the Taos Tribe* hangs today in the Smithsonian Institution, Washington, D.C. Couse's perceptions of Native Americans, portrayed in such paintings as *Braiding the Quiver*, *San Juan Pottery* and *The Lesson*, in which an Indian brave teaches his young son how to weave a blanket, project a feeling of freedom and innocence.

Couse became the favorite artist of William Simpson, advertising manager of the Atchison, Topeka and Santa Fe Railway, who purchased many of his works. They were featured on the Railway's calendars from 1914 to 1938. When the Taos Society of Artists was formed in 1915, he was elected its first president. Today, on leaving the Couse compound, one passes under a *portal* where the original six members of the Society—Couse, Phillips, Dunton, Sharp, Berninghaus and Blumenschein—posed for their formal photographs. Bidding a fond *adieu* to Paris and heading to America's Southwest paid off for E.I. Couse, who lived a life of artistic fulfillment in the Taos Valley. On April 24, 1936, his coffin was carried in solemn procession to the Sierra Vista Cemetery by his beloved Pueblo Indians.

BILL HEMP

Mabel Dodge Luhan House

"Movers and Shakers" Mix at Los Gallos

Traveling east from Taos Plaza on Kit Carson Road, then turning onto Morada Lane for a half-mile, one arrives at a cluster of dwellings clinging to a low hill at the edge of Indian land. The largest adobe is the main house, which fuses elements of pueblo, Spanish Colonial and Tuscan Villa architecture. On entering the flagstone courtyard, past massive gates decorated with sections of hand-carved balcony torn out of the Ranchos de Taos Mission Church and a quaint village of tall Mexican dovecotes just inside, the visitor is welcomed to the ultimate hacienda, *Los Gallos*, "The Roosters," the Taos estate and domain of the magnetic Mabel Ganson Evans Dodge Sterne Luhan (1879-1962).

Fleeing Victorian Buffalo, New York, after her first husband, sportsman Karl Evans, was accidentally shot and killed by a friend on a hunting trip, the 25-year old debutante daughter of wealthy Charles and Sara Ganson, offspring of two banking families, sailed the Atlantic to Europe with her small son, John. Relieved to be away from her domineering father, Mabel, aboard ship, met dapper Edwin Dodge, a Boston architect, whom she soon married and settled down with in Villa Curonia, in Florence, Italy. There they entertained such intellectuals as Bernard Berenson, Gertrude Stein and Alice B. Toklas. After a series of romantic affairs and a divorce from Dodge, Mabel returned to New York and became the chatelaine of a salon of "movers and shakers" in her Chinese-shawl-draped, stark-white apartment at 23 Fifth Avenue in Manhattan's Greenwich Village. Here she invited socialists, suffragettes, psychoanalysts and a host of creative types from around the world.

While in New York, she soon became involved in a passionate liaison with the promiscuous poet turned Red, John Reed, who later died of typhus in 1920 after serving the Communist Party in the Soviet Union. Bored with the big city, Mabel then joined her third husband, Russian-born painter and sculptor, Maurice Sterne, who had left her on a trial separation to work in New Mexico in 1917. It wasn't long before Mabel surrendered to what D. H. Lawrence later described as "the curious otherness of Taos," a village glowing like a jewel in the orange-pink light of the setting sun. Its adobe ambiance and soft undulating shapes blended in with the *chamisa* and *piñón* that dotted the plains and mountains; its air was sweet with wood smoke. Mabel's instant response to all this was "I've come home!"

In 1918, while teaching women at the pueblo how to knit, Mabel met the Tiwa Indian Antonio (Tony) Luhan, a splendid figure over six feet tall, who wore his hair in two plaits. He was always wrapped in a traditional purple blanket and was married to an Indian woman named Candelaria. His majestic stature and quiet demeanor instantly attracted Mabel. Sometime later, Tony, who had become her chauffeur, showed Mabel twelve acres of land bordered on two sides by Indian fields with an orchard on the north. Tony sent Mabel to an occultist who told her that "Taos is the beating heart of the world." The medium also advised Mabel that she was chosen to be the bridge between Indians and Anglos and that Taos was to be the center of the rebirth of the West. In June of that year, she purchased the parcel for the price of $1500 and set out to build a small four-room adobe farmhouse for her beloved land.

During the next several productive, intimate years, Mabel and Tony worked together on the place, which resulted not only in their 40-year-long and event-filled marriage but also in a rambling hodge-podge of a homestead 450 feet long. This comprised the "big room," with two *kiva* fireplaces and a ceiling supported by six hand-carved, scrolled posts chiseled by the artist Ralph Meyers; a spacious dining room, its floor covered with red-brown and black tiles polished to a high sheen with beeswax

every few days and its eye-catching ceiling constructed of saplings vividly painted in sienna red, white earth and lamp black in stripes of four to look like a Navajo blanket; and a sun-drenched kitchen where opulent, five-course meals were prepared on a big blue stove that burned cedar wood. The kitchen cupboards boasted *santos* from Mabel's prize collection. She had bought the *santos* from *Taoseños'* kitchens for one dollar each.

Extending from the main section of the hacienda to the south and hidden from the sun by a long, low *portal* accented by brightly colored ceramic roosters "crowing" on the roof, after which Mabel

named the house, are the original rooms. The library is where Mabel and Lady Dorothy Brett, the painter, spent lazy days catching up on the popular new murder mysteries of the day. Four small bedrooms have *kiva* fireplaces, diminutive doors and windows. The ceilings are constructed of *vigas* and *latillas*. Later, a second floor comprising two bedrooms was added over the big room. One was Mabel's bedroom. It had an open sleeping porch where she and Tony slept in summer on two swinging hammocks and breakfasted in the morning on toast, honey and coffee. A third-story addition served as an aerie where she could look out over her domain and the sagebrush-covered plain to the Taos Pueblo. A log cabin, built especially for her son, John Evans, with a cobblestone fireplace and chimney, was used as a schoolhouse for Mabel's grandchildren. The "Rainbow Room," so named for its pastel ceiling painted by artist friends, served as a library and a second living room. When construction was finally finished, the complex consisted of seventeen rooms covering over 8,000 square feet.

As her dwelling was transformed from farmhouse to hacienda, the bright, gray-eyed Mabel, who wore her thick chestnut hair in bangs, Pueblo-style, came to view the people of the ancient Taos

Pueblo as a living organism of nature, art and community. Consequently, the task for the rest of her life was to promote these redemptive values by drawing a continuing flow of creative people to the climate and culture of New Mexico. In her letters she painted Taos as the Garden of Eden, attracting a host of powerful people. Ansel Adams, photographer, spent his life focusing his camera on the West. Willa Cather, during her fortnight stay, was so impressed by Tony Luhan that, when creating the Navajo Indian, Eusabio, in *Death Comes for the Archbishop,* she drew essentially from his character. Georgia O'Keeffe, the ascetic, aloof artist, painted erotic, larger-than-life flora, sun-bleached steer skulls decorated with desert flowers and vivid pink southwestern cliffs. Irritated with Mabel, O'Keeffe finally fled to the pastel-hued bluffs of Abiquiu.

A festive dinner party at the famous hostess's domain might find an invited guest rubbing elbows with Thomas Wolfe, Thornton Wilder, Aldous Huxley, Carl Jung, Edward Hopper and Mary Austin. Lady Dorothy Brett remembered Mabel's dining room as the scene of Indian dances staged for dinner guests and delicious food served by her handsome Indian maid, Albidia. "She gave Indian dances in her dining room. They would undress in the kitchen and they would come in dancing in their dance costumes. Perfectly beautiful!" Brett said. Her prize catch, however, was D. H. Lawrence, the English author, whom she hoped would write the great American novel and cast her as the heroine. While staying at the hacienda with his wife, Frieda, who was suspicious of Mabel's intentions, Lawrence was so shocked by the lack of privacy in the bathroom on the second floor with windows on three sides, he decided to

(Drawing of Mabel Dodge Luhan after a sketch by Nicolai Fechin in the collection of the University of New Mexico Museum.)

paint colorful designs on the windowpanes, blocking any views by outsiders to the interior. Like them or not, Lawrence's artistic brush strokes can be seen to this very day. Exasperated by her luxurious lifestyle, D. H. pressed Mabel into scrubbing the floors in the kitchen and doing other menial tasks. Fed up with his antics, she shipped the Lawrences up to her ranch on Lobo Mountain.

During the 1940s life was quiet in the American Southwest while World War II raged in Europe and the South Pacific. "Peg," as Mabel was called by close friends, ordered a smaller adobe residence built for her adjacent to the big house. She left the hacienda behind. It was later bought by the actor Dennis Hopper. In 1937, Mabel donated *La Posta*, the casa she had built for her son, John, to the Sisters of Loretto as a convent. Today, some *Taoseños* say *La Posta* is haunted. In her later years, Mabel took the lead in building Holy Cross Hospital in Taos, continued to support the work of local artists and writers and donated hundreds of books to the Harwood Library. During her life she penned a great number of memoirs, most notably *Edge of the Taos Desert* and *Winter in Taos*, which captured the essence of the valley.

On August 18, 1962, Mabel Dodge died of coronary thrombosis at the age of 83, and was buried in the Kit Carson Cemetery in Taos. Her husband, Tony, passed away shortly afterward and was interred in the graveyard at the Taos Pueblo on the site of the original San Gerónimo Chapel. Spud Johnson, who served as Mabel's secretary and also published a glossy little magazine, *Laughing Horse*, wrote a number of stories about Mabel, but the full story of her life, amid all those "movers and shakers" remains to be written.

La Morada de Don Fernando de Taos
The Prayerful Brotherhood of the Penitentes

From the early Spanish Colonial days until 1921, there has existed in Taos a sect known as *Los Hermanos Penitentes*. This Third Order of St. Francis was the last in a long line of laymen who led exemplary lives but believed in public whipping and carrying the *madero,* cross, for self-discipline during *La Cuaresma*, the Lenten Season. They felt it was important to emulate Christ's painful experience in order to gain entrance into heaven. It is believed that the first Christian to flog himself was St. Pardulf, a Benedictine monk, in the year 737 A.D. This so impressed other Christians that by 1056 A.D., flagellation in southern Europe was quite common. When Don Juan de Oñate explored north from Old Mexico in 1598, he brought with him Franciscan priests, who indulged in self-punishment. The priests were to preach the faith and convert the Indians. As a result, Taos, for years, maintained the most powerful meeting place, *La Morada de Fernando de Taos*, built circa 1860. It crouches in the desert on Pueblo Indian land, adjacent to a *camposanto,* cemetery, on Las Cruces Lane.

For the *Penitentes*, Easter Season was the time, when as ardent believers in Christ's words "Take up thy cross and follow Me," they recreated the Stations of the Cross and the suffering and death of Jesus at Calvary. Their bodies bare except for short, thin, white cotton undergarments called *calzones* and their faces hidden behind black *vendas*, hoods, they formed a procession. The purpose was to emulate Christ on the cross by hanging a living man, one of their own, on the crude wooden cross. All the men carried *disciplinas*, whips made from loosely plaited yucca fibre plants. As they moved silently, without a cry of pain, in procession, the whips would drop forward, then be brought back with great power, smashing against their backs. Before the punishment even began, the participant's backs had been slashed with three crosses by a sharpened flint or a shard of glass. Another common form of penance was to drag the extremely heavy, wooden *madero*, which was taller than a man. Because of the weight of the cross, the procession often had to be halted at short intervals to allow for the *acompañadores* to lift the *madero* from the shoulders of the *Penitentes* and permit them to recuperate their strength.

The honored individual selected to represent Christ would carry the cross up into a mountain canyon, sometimes in heavy snow drifts, taxing his strength. On rare occasions, the man would die while still bound by ropes to the cross. When his shoes were left at his wife's or mother's doorstep, she knew immediately that her husband or son had made the supreme sacrifice.

In the early days of the 20th century, there were a number of *moradas* within 100 miles of Taos, in villages like Las Trampas and Truchas, where symbolic crucifixions did take place. In 1889, when the Vatican in Rome finally banned the organization, which had been vehemently despised by the French Archbishop Jean Baptiste Lamy of Santa Fe, the *Penitentes* went underground. Great caution was then taken to ensure the safety of the brother, or *hermano*, who impersonated Christ. In almost every *morada*, up until 1921, there continued the ritual of praying, chanting, singing and whipping with a yucca scourge.

The *Penitentes* dragged their cumbersome burden from the *morada* along the snow-banked road. Branches of forked rattlesnake cactus were tightly bound to their naked backs and chests with ropes. The Lenten procession followed. At the lead was the *sangrador* carrying a life-size *bulto* of the bleeding Christ, or an *anda*, a litter bearing a statue of the Blessed Mother. Alongside the *sangrador* walked the *rezador,* or reader, chanting the ritual. The *rezador* was accompanied by the *pitero*, whose small wooden flute, the *pito*, produced shrill wailing notes. Then came two men with *matrakas*, wooden rattles. Several *hermanos* acted as guards. They were followed by the cross-bearers, who staggered with tortured steps. All finally reached the distant *Calvario*.

One *Penitente* was given the task of dragging the *Carreta del Muerto*, Death Cart, by a horse-hair rope passed over his shoulders and beneath his armpits. The weight of the cart dug into his naked flesh. The main procession of *Penitentes*, following in the footsteps of the cross-bearers, chanted old *alabados,* or hymns. Although they could not be active mem-

Drawing of Death Cart after Carreta del Muerto in the Millicent Rogers Museum.

bers of the *Penitentes*, the Spanish women would bring food—a sweet porridge-like substance consisting of sprouted wheat flour, brown sugar and honey. When boiled and baked in an outdoor oven, this porridge became thick as jam, called *panocha*. They also prepared *atole*, a blue-corn-meal concoction made into a thick drink. Partaking of these, the participants gained the necessary strength to bear the ordeal of the scourging and cross bearing.

With spring arriving late in Taos and Easter falling early, the *Penitentes* usually had to make their Lenten journey through cold winds and deep snow. These pilgrimages took on a mystical tapestry—barefooted men bearing the burden of the dead weight of their crosses; the blindfolded *Cristo* in red dress; braided yucca whips lashing at bare shoulders; the strange sound of rattles, sheets of tin and the clanking of chains; the faces of the *hermano's* followers showing utter exhaustion; the weird cries and groans of anguish; the pale-faced elderly women in black *rebozos* looking like the death figure of *Doña Sevastania* on the Death Cart. All were players in a pageant from a bygone century.

In the early years of the Spanish settlements, most villages in northern New Mexico could not have a resident priest. There simply were not enough clergy to supply the demand. They did have the close-knit brotherhood of the *Penitentes*. In those days, the people in these remote villages were often in grave danger from Indian attacks. No help was available except their faith in God. So the altruistic brotherhood kept the faith alive by conducting prayer services, tending the sick, saying the rosary, and assisting in burying the dead. What's more, out of their zeal grew the only American-born art form not extant when the Spaniards arrived in the New World. These were called *santos*, *retablos* and *bultos*, depicting saints and revered personages of the church. They were fashioned from cedar wood that grew in the region. These *santos* are coated with gesso and painted with vegetable

dyes gathered from the fields, along with pulverized clay, rock and black from the charcoal of hearth fires. Today, these *santos* grace the churches, *capillas* and museums throughout the Taos Valley.

As each chapter built its meetinghouse in accordance with existing construction materials and the local site, *morada* architecture became, by no means, uniform. During the 1600s and 1700s, most *moradas* had flat, earthen roofs, distinguished by their compact, low-lying silhouette. This is especially true of the Taos Morada, with its warm-colored adobe walls of a truly organic quality. The structure's massiveness seems all the more emphatic because of the

paucity of openings. There are only a front door and several small windows. Of the structure's two rooms, the largest room served as a chapel with an altar surrounded by a railing where during Passion Week a *velorio,* or wake, for the saints was held. The smaller room was used as a meeting place and storeroom. Here, the Taos *Hermanos* gathered about a fireplace to take meals and carry on discussions when not involved in prayer and religious observances.

In 1947, the fervent brotherhood of *Penitentes* was welcomed back into the Catholic Church by Edwin Byrnes, Archbishop of the Santa Fe Diocese, as a result of their promise to forgo the ancient rite of flagellation.

The lonely Don Fernando de Taos Morada is reached by walking over a wooden bridge across a fast-flowing *acequia*. The wind whistles down from the Sangre de Cristo Mountains and whips across a stark white cross, punctuating the far distance. The wanderer can almost hear the shrill-sounding wail of the *pito* as it sends a cold shiver down the spine. One can almost make out, far down the path studded with wild rabbit-brush, the gray, ghostlike figures of *Los Hermanos Penitentes* making their reverential stations of the Cross.

Guadalupe Plaza

Padre Martínez: Priest, Publisher and Politician

In the year 1610, church bells pealed across the Taos Valley. Franciscan friars accompanied the Spanish *conquistadores* and established the Mission of San Gerónimo, led by Fray Francisco de Zamora. It served not only the Indians of the Pueblo but also the first Spanish settlers with names like Luhan, Miranda and Ramos, who lived on ranches, called *estancias*. Sadly, the bells stopped ringing in 1680 when the Indians revolted against the Spaniards, killing the missionaries, destroying the church and driving the settlers south to Old Mexico.

When Don Diego de Vargas was chosen by the Viceroy of New Spain to make a reconquest of New Mexico in 1692, the Indians then established friendly relations with the new wave of Spanish settlers and began the restoration of the Church of San Gerónimo de Taos. Happily, bells rang again in the verdant valley calling worshipers to Mass. With thriving missions at the pueblo and the Church of San Francisco de Asís at Ranchos, the citizens of Don Fernando de Taos petitioned Bishop Olivares of Durango to allow them to establish a mission church of their own. Permission was granted to construct a church in honor of Our Lady of Guadalupe. The mission was built afterwards with massive adobe walls and a single tower topped by a cross. In 1826, the church's first native-born priest, Don Antonio Jose Martínez y Santistevan, took over as pastor of Our Lady of Guadalupe, one of the first parishes in the United States to be dedicated to the Patroness of the New World, the Queen of All the Americas.

Today, over a century and a quarter after the passing of Padre Martínez, the question is still asked about this truly remarkable figure in Taos history: was he a saint to be revered or a devil in black robes? The son of an influential rancher, Martínez was born January 10, 1793 in Abiquiu. The family moved to Taos in 1804, where young Antonio did a man's work, tilling soil and herding sheep on the huge hacienda. In 1812, at age nineteen, he married his boyhood sweetheart, Maria de la Luz Martínez of Abiquiu. Just a short year later, she died after giving birth to a daughter, Luz. Broken hearted, Don Antonio turned to the priesthood, left his daughter in the care of his loving parents and embarked for Durango, Mexico, where he entered the Tridentine Seminary.

Alive with intellectual curiosity and excelling in many subjects—theology, philosophy and canon law—Martínez was awarded several scholarships. One was a *Beca Real*, Royal Scholarship, which supported him until his ordination in February of 1822. Returning to Taos in 1826, the padre opened a school in his adobe home, which produced a new generation of New Mexico clergy. It stands today on Padre Martínez Lane, west of Guadalupe Plaza, where his descendants still reside. In 1835, he established a printing press, one of the first in New Mexico and west of the Mississippi. On this press, Martínez published a newspaper with the masthead, *El Crespúsculo de la Libertad*, the Dawn of Liberty. His rationale for starting up the publication was "to clip the wings of my opponents."

Limited in his command of the English language but most knowledgeable in all aspects of government and civil and canon law, Martínez had firsthand experience in the social problems of his native New Mexico. He opposed the Maxwell Land Grant, which he saw as a land grab by U.S. newcomers. That opposition made him enemies among the *Americanos* of Santa Fe, especially Archbishop Jean Baptiste Lamy (1814-1888). Extremely jealous of the padre's popularity with Spanish Americans, Lamy demanded excessive tithes of the Taos parish, which threatened in some cases to withhold sacraments from church members who did not pay 10 percent of their income. At the same time, the archbishop despised Martínez's involvement with the *Hermanos Penitentes* and their "barbaric rite of flagellation." A stranger in a strange land, Lamy tried to "Frenchify" the local Spaniards and civilize the rustic New Mexicans. In addition, he made every attempt possible to excommunicate and unfrock Padre Martínez for his involvement with the *Penitentes* as well as his political activities. But, according to church records, there is no evidence the archbishop ever followed through with the formal canonical process; therefore, it appears that the padre was never excommunicated.

(Drawing of Padre Martínez after a photograph courtesy of the Church of Our Lady of Guadalupe.)

On a bitter-cold morning in January 1847, a revolt led by Pablo Montoya, a Mexican, exploded in Taos. Padre Martínez was awakened by a terrified crowd of people in his *plazuela* screaming, "Open, for the love of God, open! The Indians and Mexicans are killing Don Carlos Bent, Don Luís Lee and others!" The priest opened his door and bade the desperate group to come in. He gave them food and provided arms to sentries who stood guard on the rooftop against the attackers, who kept screaming "Traitors, traitors!" Soon after, the padre sent an urgent message advising Colonel Sterling Price of the situation. Arriving in Taos on February 15, the colonel was given lodgings at the Martínez home. The next day, Price and his troops marched north to the Indian Pueblo and opened fire on the San Gerónimo Church, sending salvo after salvo into the ancient edifice-turned-fortress. After three days of combat, the holed-up Indians and Mexicans surrendered. Days later, the court-martial and prosecution of Montoya and his men by the colonel was carried out in the padre's home. Those who accused the priest of complicity with the insurgents proved to be wrong.

Padre Martínez answered all the accusations against him with his mighty pen. In his last will and testament, he wrote, ". . . and my body shall descend calmly into the silence of the grave, and my soul will ascend and face the Divine Tribunal with the full knowledge and satisfaction that I did all within my power to elevate the minds of my fellow citizens . . . my conscience is at peace." On July 27, 1867, he died quietly after forty-two years of spiritual ministering and a storm-tossed political life in his beloved land.

His marble headstone in Kit Carson Cemetery, cut in Spanish, reads "The Legislature of the Territory at the time of his death called him the 'Honor of his Country.'" Vincente Martínez, the padre's great-great grandson, contends that he is not convinced the remains buried in the *camposanto* are those of the historic prelate. "He requested that he be buried under his *oratorio*, which might mean his study. We may be standing over his grave," Martínez declared in the padre's home. "I think history has proven him to be truly a great leader and a man way beyond his time," he added.

In 1911, with the original church desperately in need of repairs, the Archbishop of Santa Fe ordered Father Joseph Giraud, the pastor, to build a new edifice on the plaza site. Fifty years later, in 1961, this second church was set afire by young boys searching with matches for pigeon eggs in the darkened belfry. Within a year, a new church of Our Lady of Guadalupe was dedicated. Built of adobe in modern pueblo style with a single front tower, the church holds within its walls a treasury of religious art. In the main sanctuary stands a magnificent altar screen designed by Roberto Lavadie. It depicts the six *capillas* that support the main church in the Taos Valley. To the left of the sanctuary hangs a huge painting of Nuestra Señora de Guadalupe as she appeared to a poor Indian shepherd, Juan Diego, on Tepeyec Hill outside of Mexico City, December 9, 1531. He was canonized a saint by Pope John Paul II in 1994. The dramatic canvas painted by the artist R. William Couch complements the Stations of the Cross carved by *santero* Pedro Chavez. With its stout *viga* ceiling, main altar floor with colorful tiles and glowing stained glass windows inset with abstract designs, the church on Guadalupe Plaza is well worthy of a visit.

For worshippers in Taos, the Christmas holidays begin on December 12, the feast day of Our Lady of Guadalupe. At this time, candlelight processions are led by the Rev. Edmund Savilla, the pastor and a Native American. The frosty night is lighted by *luminarias*, or bonfires, consisting of stacks of fragrant *piñón* logs. At each station, represented by one of the six *capillas*, and the main church, prayers are said and displays of dazzling fireworks are set off in joyful celebration. Lining the rooftop of the church, the twinkling lights of *farolitos* softly glow. These are small candles anchored in sand inside brown paper bags placed a few feet apart. They cast a romantic quality on the northern New Mexican night. "*Feliz Navidad y Prospero Año Nuevo*" is the warm greeting that resounds around historic Guadalupe Plaza. The old padre would be pleased to bestow his blessing on such a joyous event.

The Navajo Gallery

R. C. Gorman: Native American, Artistic Workhorse

In the summer of 1964, Rudolph Carl Gorman, a Navajo Indian on the move up the artistic ladder in the San Francisco Bay area, visited Taos for the first time. He found himself off the beaten track on Ledoux Street, in front of the Manchester Gallery. This historic adobe was once the home and studio of artist Eleanora Kissel. Sauntering into the gallery, he met the owner, John Manchester, who on seeing his work, offered Gorman a one-man exhibition the next year. Thus began the amazingly successful career of R.C. Gorman, as he likes to be called, and the celebrated studio in Taos that he promptly renamed the Navajo Gallery, after his own people.

Imaginative, outgoing and gregarious, Gorman opened his fledgling gallery in the late 1960s. It was a parade of imaginative artists, poets and creative children of the "Flower Generation," as this was the era of the "hippies" in Taos. A visitor to the Navajo Gallery would not only be swept away by the artist's natural sociability but also be astonished at the display of his art on the walls: canvases splashed with his wild, vivid memories of Navajo rug designs and pueblo pottery chards and colorful portraits of earthy Indian women in their brightly striped blankets.

Gorman was born in 1932, during the Depression, at Chinle, Arizona, near Canyon de Chelly. His youthful years were taken up in an individual struggle against prejudice and poverty. Endowed with a heritage rich in the culture of generations of his own people—silversmiths, sand painters, holy men and tribal leaders—as a child he made his first paintings with sand and rocks on the earthen floor of the hogan where he lived. Attending a one-room schoolhouse in Chinle, R.C. received an initial recognition for his artistic talents by drawing a "naked" lady and being promptly spanked on the backside by both his teacher and his mother.

During Gorman's high school years, a volunteer teacher, Miss Jenny Lind, who quickly recognized the boy's talents, encouraged and allowed the young Navajo freedom to experiment. After attending Northern Arizona University in Flagstaff in 1958, R.C. won the first scholarship ever given by the Navajo tribe for study outside the United States. At the College of Mexico in Mexico City, he was introduced to the fabulous works of such outstanding Mexican artists as Diego Rivera, José Orozco and David Siqueiros. Each of them made a monumental impact on Gorman's creative thinking. In Mexico he found his unique style and was introduced to the medium of lithography, which has become an important facet of his work.

Following his artistic tenure in Mexico, Gorman moved on to San Francisco,where he opened a studio and started painting full time. He experimented with just about every possible style, all the while supporting himself by joining the Model's Guild and becoming a successful male nude model. In 1972, his first lithograph suite, *Homage to a Navajo Woman*, was published by the Tamarind Institute. It became an instant success. By 1973,

New York's Metropolitan Museum of Art included him as the only living Native American painter in their "American Indian Art" exhibit, bringing him increasing national recognition.

Once settled into the gallery on Ledoux Street, where he also lived, Gorman painted and personally interacted with an ever-increasing flow of patrons. Gallery hours were unusually relaxed and impromptu. If R.C. wasn't home, there might be a polite note posted on the front door instructing visitors where to find him— "Join me at El Patio Restaurant on Teresina Lane." If one happened by the warm-lighted gallery at the end of a busy business day,

there was always the possibility of being invited by the artist to stay for a five-course dinner. He is known far and wide as an outstanding gourmet chef.

By 1979, finding it difficult to concentrate on his drawings, paintings and sculptures and run an art gallery in the same place, Gorman purchased an old adobe dwelling clutching a high ridge in the countryside north of Taos on the road to Questa. There he constructed an enormous studio with an inspiring view of Taos Mountain. The Navajo artist filled the new additions of his walled compound with the works of world-renowned artists such as Chagall,

Picasso, Rory Wagner and Georgia O'Keeffe. Today, as during his early career, Indian women—earthy, stoic, enigmatic, beautiful—dominate Gorman's work. He said, "Women are a constant challenge because their infinite variety invites an infinity of interpretations. I have a preference for the ample woman. Her figure occupies space softly, and I must work from live models. I draw energy from them. The model sets the mood. If she's sour, it shows. If she's spontaneous and alive, so is my work."

In describing his self-portrait on canvas, Gorman commented: "I don't think a creative person can visualize himself as anything else. I have done everything. I've been a dishwasher, a busboy. I've been in the U.S. Navy. All the time I have been an artist."

Regarding his mixed-media 1968 painting, *Premonition*, in the collection of the painter, Gorman said, "I have used pottery and rug motifs in some of my series, because I know that before long there will be no more Indians and no more of his crafts and arts. We will finally be obliterated by total integration. And all that we were will be lost forever."

Angelina, his bronze sculpture created in 1977, exemplifies his talent as a sculptor and his love of women with big hands and strong feet who work on the land. Gorman explained, "I deal with the common woman who smells of the fields and maize. She lives and breathes. She's human."

R. C. Gorman, the premier artist among Native American Indians, has gone through many phases in his career: paintings, landscapes, surreal series, pottery, rug and mask series. More recent extensions of his talents include etchings, silk-screens, sculpture, ceramics and tapestries. The New York Times called Gorman "The Picasso of Native Americans." As he is prolific, profitable, philanthropic and a delight to all who know him, his Navajo Gallery on Ledoux in Taos draws *aficianados* from near and far. And, of course, well into the far-distant future.

(Drawing of R.C. Gorman after a photograph courtesy of the Navajo Gallery.)

Blumenschein
STUDIO

HOME & MUSEUM
ERNEST BLUMENSCHEIN
CO-FOUNDER OF THE
TAOS SOCIETY OF ARTISTS

BILL HEMP

Ernest Blumenschein Home and Museum

Bert, "Blumy" and a Broken Wagon Wheel

Situated on narrow, serpentine Ledoux Street, named for two French fur trappers, Abraham and Antoine, the Blumenschein Home, parts of which date from 1797, can be described as an art museum with a homelike ambiance. The co-founder of the legendary Taos Society of Artists, Ernest L. Blumenschein, purchased this masterpiece of an adobe dwelling from a fellow artist, W. Herbert "Buck" Dunton, in 1919, after spending many summers in Taos, away from New York. The European antique furnishings and the work of this talented family of artists—Ernest, his wife, Mary Shepherd Greene, and their daughter, Helen—along with paintings of other prominent Taos artists, such as Bert Geer Phillips, Oscar Berninghaus and Leon Gaspard, carry the visitor back to an earlier era of art and culture in the Taos Valley.

While studying at the Académie Julian in Paris in 1895, Ernest Blumenschein and his good friend, Bert Phillips, met artist Joseph Henry Sharp, who described in vivid detail his visit to Taos, New Mexico, in 1893 and encouraged them to travel there and paint at the first opportunity. They embarked in 1898 on a leisurely sketching trip from Denver intended to end in Mexico. A rear wheel on their lightweight, horse-drawn surrey slipped into a deep rut on a miserable mountain trail and broke. Since the nearest blacksmith was probably about thirty miles south in the village of Taos, the pair decided to flip a three-dollar gold coin—the only money they had to their name—to determine who would take the damaged

wheel into the valley. "Blumy," who lost the toss, set out on horseback with the broken wheel in tow, leaving Phillips behind to keep watch over their precious art supplies, wagon and the other horse. As he approached the Taos Valley, Ernest became suddenly spellbound by the pastel-shaded mountains, the brilliant desert light and the Pueblo Indians draped in brightly colored blankets and shawls. Once the wheel was repaired at Bill Hinde's Blacksmith Shop, Blumy returned to Bert with news that there was painting material in Taos as exotic as anything Paul Gauguin had found in Tahiti. On his arrival in the valley, Phillips was equally enchanted and the twosome decided to stay put and paint.

In the years that followed, more artists arrived in Taos, having gotten word about the valley from Bert and Blumy in conversations at the Salmagundi Club in Manhattan, where the two shared a studio. Then, in 1915, Blumenschein and Sharp, both Ohioans; Phillips, a New Yorker; Berninghaus, a St. Louisan; E. Irving Couse of Michigan, and Dunton, from Maine, became the six founders of the famous Taos Society of Artists. Its purpose was to enable the members as a group to exhibit their art in various galleries throughout the country. Victor Higgins, from Indiana, and Walter Ufer, a Kentuckian, were added to the original six who established Taos as an internationally known art center. In subsequent decades, the Taos artists painted the Southwest with vigor and affection. With the financial support of the Santa Fe Railroad, which for years featured their paintings in its national advertising campaigns, along with the success of their traveling exhibits, the society had its reputation made from the Atlantic to the Pacific.

It was in Paris that Blumenschein met his future wife, Mary Greene, five years his senior. She was also an accomplished artist. Mary did numerous illustrations for books and magazines and was greatly influenced by the Impressionists with whom she had studied in France. Her work, which demonstrates a softer palette, focused mostly on feminine subjects. When the young couple purchased the property in 1919 and moved permanently from New York, their house consisted of only four rooms. But as neighbors living in adjacent quarters moved away, the Blumenscheins bought them up until they eventually owned twelve rooms, while converting Buck Dunton's studio into a garage and rooms for storage. The artists brought with them to New Mexico many fine pieces of antique furniture picked up on their travels in Europe. To these were added handmade Taos furniture and carved antiques from Mexico. After moving to Taos, Mary turned to designing silver jewelry in an attempt to placate Blumy's temper; the marriage to Ernest was a source of both mental anguish and inspiration. Helen, their only child, like her parents, studied art in Paris. She went on to continue the family's artistic tradition, distinguishing herself with her portraits, line drawings and charcoal sketches, as well as delving into archeology.

Entering the courtyard and walking past a small stable that houses a bombazine black, fringe-topped surrey, similar to the one that broke down on the trail to Taos, the visitor is drawn to a rustic outdoor well with a wooden roof surrounded by cosmos, zinnias, daisies and hollyhocks in a riot of color. This was a favorite gathering place and breakfast nook for the Blumenscheins, who were noted for their good taste, talent and unpretentiousness.

Strolling inside the adobe structure through the book-lined gift shop and the cozy kitchen, one arrives in the old world dining room, which displays Indian works of art collected by the Blumenscheins from the 1920s through the 1940s. These artists, most of whom were self-taught, were the fathers of Modern Indian Art, having started their careers painting on cardboard boxes or pottery. The low couch by the front door is a "Taos Bed," handmade during the 1930s as part of a WPA project. In the library, lined with rare volumes, a guest in the house-museum discovers an exotic collection of Japanese art given to the family by students from Japan whom Ernest had instructed while in New York. Looking out the windows of the library one can catch a glimpse of the Río de Don Fernando, the original watering hole of Taos, where town women congregated to wash their clothes; it later became the first fish hatchery in Taos.

In the spacious studio, with its high ceiling and tall windows enlarged for more light, are hung major works by Ernest and Mary. *St. Francis Church*, which sits on a trusty easel next to the adobe fireplace that is crowned by an old Spanish crucifix, serves as a classic example of Ernest's brush work. The canvas also demonstrates the artistic license a painter can take. This view of the celebrated Ranchos de Taos Mission is not really accurate in that there are no mountains to the west behind the church and the cloaked figures suggest the Pueblo Indians, who would more likely have attended the little Church of San Gerónimo at their multitiered pueblo. Ernest's *Railway Yard-Meeting Called* and

Alas, Proud Mountain are two treasures of his time spent in Albuquerque in the 1950s. Mary Greene's painting, *Girl with Fan*, hanging behind the wood stove in the studio, demonstrates her use of much softer hues.

The exhibit room at the rear of the house contains the Kit Carson Historic Museum's eclectic collection of Taos art. Works by Phillips, Sharp and Ufer and other members of the Taos Society of Artists hang on the far wall. Works by later artists include those of Leon Gaspard, who painted the *trastero*, cupboard, with Persian scenes; Ila McAfee, who made a career of painting horses; and Rebecca Salsbury James, best known for her reverse paintings on glass such as *White Roses at Twilight*.

Ernest Blumenschein's approach to Indian subjects was forceful and direct. He possessed an intellectual grasp of the mystical aspect of the Native American consciousness and successfully applied it to canvases, while conveying the strength of the Indian character. Blumy, in all his years in Taos, dedicated himself faithfully to rendering the personal and human side of the Pueblo Indian as a noble individual.

The rambling, twelve-room Spanish home, which blends the sophistication of European charm with the tranquil beauty of the classical Taos architectural style, has been lovingly restored to its original mud-plaster adobe, inside and out. The building and courtyard, now one of the Kit Carson Museums and designated a National Historic Landmark, serves to memorialize a gifted painter who discovered the Taos Valley just by chance and remained to create an artistic legacy. One wonders what would have happened if the wheel on Bert and Blumy's wagon had never broken on that rutted road above Taos.

BILL HEMP

The Harwood Foundation Museum

Elizabeth's Lending Library Becomes a Magnet of Wisdom

Situated at the west end of Ledoux Street, within walking distance of the plaza, on a high ridge where adobe dwellings were first built in the early 1800s, snuggles one of the most beloved buildings in all of Taos, known to townspeople as "The Harwood." Since the 1920s this historic compound has served as a museum, library and meeting place, attracting residents and visitors alike. The complex's origin and history are tightly woven into the artistic and literary heritage of Taos and its people.

The original structure was acquired by Captain Smith H. Simpson, who came West to serve in a military campaign against the Ute Indians, arriving in Taos in 1859. He later served as confidential clerk for the nearly illiterate Kit Carson. Later, he served as an officer during the Civil War. Simpson designed the house in the typical Taos manner with *vigas* and *latillas* and plastered it with adobe mud. After his death in 1916, his heirs sold their family home for $1200 to Burrit Elihu Harwood (1857-1922) and his wife, Lucy Case (1867-1938). Lucy was known by everybody in Taos as Elizabeth. "Burt" Harwood was an artist and avid photographer. While living in France and suffering from tuberculosis, he heard about the quaint village in northern New Mexico. He decided to retire there, paint and take pictures in an atmosphere congenial to his way of life.

The Harwoods acquired additional land on both sides of their new home and set about establishing their complex. They called it *El Pueblito*, the little village, since its design was strongly influenced by the Taos Pueblo—a classical blend of Pueblo Indian and Spanish traditions. Their house became the first residential building to support a second story and to have its own electrical generating system. The house was unique in that some of its walls of solid adobe bulged to a thickness of more than six feet.

Dorothy Berninghaus Brandenburg, daughter of the artist Oscar Berninghaus, recalls that the Harwoods, on settling in Taos, were astonished to learn that the village had no public library. "When their building developed sufficiently, Elizabeth opened a lending library from her front *portal* and sat there several mornings each week in the summers to issue books from their extensive personal collection. This became very popular. As a lovely and gracious gesture from the librarian, you were served iced tea as you checked out your book." Dorothy added, "Here began our first library."

In November 1923, a year after Burt's death, Elizabeth Harwood joined with friends Victor Higgins, Bert Phillips, T.P. Martin, William Frayne and B.G. Randall to create what would become one of New Mexico's most enduring arts institutions. The Harwood Foundation, first established as a private nonprofit organization, would in 1935, in a "Deed of Conveyance" signed by Elizabeth, transfer ownership of the Harwood property to the University of New Mexico.

The main library and art gallery, constructed in 1938 as a Depression-era project, were designed by the noted architect of the Pueblo Revival period, John Gaw Meem. Placed on the National Register of Historic Places in 1976, the entire building complex was extensively renovated. Today, the Harwood consists of three libraries: the General Collection, the Padre Martínez Special Collection and the Taos Children's Library. The main library, containing over 35,000 volumes, constitutes an exceptional public library collection for a town the size of Taos. Built in 1971, the Imhof Reading Room holds the library's reference materials, current periodicals and the circulating Southwest Collection.

Housed on the second floor of the building, the Harwood Foundation Museum of Taos Arts, the crown jewel of the complex, consists of about 1,000 paintings, prints, drawings and sculptures by over 100 artists. According to the *Harwood Foundation's Brief History and Collection Listing* (1923-1993), it all began one day in the mid-1930s, when Victor Higgins, who had been moved by the funeral of a young boy killed in an automobile accident, walked into the Harwood with a large canvas tucked under his arm. He announced to the awed curator: "Here is a painting for over the fireplace." Thus, did the Harwood secure its most important picture, *Winter Funeral*, with the stark, snow-covered mountains dwarfing the dark-clad mourners and their little cortege of wagons in the valley. Other master-works one can admire in the collection are *Santiago, The War Chief* by Oscar E. Berninghaus, *Autumn Fruit* by Andrew Dasburg, *The Taos Indians* by Leon Gaspard, *Navajo Mother and Child* by E. Martin Hennings, *Christmas Eve at Taos Pueblo* by Gene Kloss, *Winter in New Mexico* by Walter Ufer, *Taos Ten Out to Lunch* by Jim Wagner and John Young-Hunter's *Portrait of Mabel Dodge Luhan*.

Under the direction of Willard "Spud" Johnson and later Toni Tarleton, in the years from 1954 to 1972, and spurred by their intense determination and devotion to the Harwood, the collection increased steadily in books, money and art. Toni encouraged local artists and collectors to donate pictures and other art, thus expanding the fine collection enjoyed today.

Over the years, the Harwood provided three functions to the town of Taos. One was its use as a community center for meetings, classes and performances. Another was its role as the public library in Taos, the focus of Harwood programs for decades. Established in June 1926, the library was proved popular from its start with the community, which generously supports the growth of its collections. The single most important patron was Mabel Dodge Luhan, who for years made sure the library was kept stocked with bestsellers and literary classics. The third role was to serve as display space for the visual arts. Art has been shown in every nook and cranny of the Harwood. Even into the 1950s, the library was decorated with clay pots and other Indian artifacts, Hispanic textiles, Patrocino Barela's wood carvings, 19th century *retablos* and a cannonball said to have come from the 1847 bombardment of Taos Pueblo by Union troops.

The special collections of the Harwood are safely stored in locked cases and contain invaluable volumes on the anthropology, history and fine arts of the Southwest. These include a rare Spanish grammar printed in Taos in 1837 under the direction of Padre Martínez on a press taken over the Santa Fe Trail on oxen-pulled carts and *Taos Pueblo*, a volume of Ansel Adams' dramatic black and white photographs, inscribed by the author "For Mabel and Tony Luhan."

Behind its vine-covered, ocher-hued adobe walls, with silvery-gray Russian olive trees floating above, the beloved Harwood serves every day as the central nucleus of the Taos creative community. John Nichols, the popular author and artist, whose twenty-two etchings titled *Calaveras* are to be found in the Harwood Collection of Art, wrote these words about the place:

"I love the Harwood in springtime, when apple blossoms are replete in the courtyard. And I have always loved it in winter when snow is gently falling at twilight. The Harwood draws me the way a good old small-town magnet draws the soul: promising wisdom, comfort, a familiar respite from the storm."

BILL HEMP

La Loma Plaza Historic District
An Ancient Bastion Beckons "Buck" and "Bernie"

On the first of May in the year 1796, sixty-three Spanish settler families appeared before the Don Fernando de Taos *alcalde*, Antonio Jose Ortiz, petitioning for land outside the old town limits on which to establish a new village. The mayor told them that if they were to settle there the land must have sufficient water. The site also had to be situated high on a hill with nearby pastures on which to raise crops and tend livestock. What's more, they would be required to guard themselves with firearms against possible attacks by marauding Comanche and Ute Indians. He sternly added that if they did not provide for their safety, they were "to be ejected from said settlement."

The settlers followed the *alcalde's* demands to the very letter. All the homes they soon built were one-story adobes with peeled pine logs forming the basis of the earthen roofs. Each one connected to the other to form a square bastion. Each dwelling had one or two rooms with a door and a shuttered window facing the inner plaza. Thus was created the fortified village of La Plazuela de San Antonio, the "Little Plaza of Saint Anthony."

In that same year, Spain officially recognized the tiny hilltop settlement as one of the first plazas in New Mexico formed after the governor's edict that all such places be constructed as fortified villages. A century and a half later, in the year 1964, it was renamed La Loma, the hill, when the community created a little park in the center of the sloping square. This was originally used by settlers as a corral for livestock when the animals were brought inside the walls at night after grazing in the green pastures outside.

Today, as the visitor does a turn around La Loma Plaza, the scene consists of adobe buildings forming a complete square between Ranchitos Road on the south and San Antonio on the north. The diminutive Chapel of San Antonio on the northeast side is next to the only entrance into the compound.

The plaza was built on land donated in the early 19th century by Inocencio Valdes, Jr. The charming *capilla*, with its Taos blue doors and squat bell tower, is the scene of joyous celebrations in June to mark San Antonio's Feast Day. While many early settlements in northern New Mexico originated as fortified plazas, La Loma stands as one of the only two in the state that are still residential; the other is the picturesque but crumbling Plaza del Cerro in Chimayó, built circa 1680.

In the quaint, cobbled La Loma Historic District still reside many proud descendants of the original settlers who moved here back in 1796: the Jaramillo, Martínez, Trujillo, Espinoza and Valdés families, to mention just a few. Driving up steep Valdés Lane to the ancient enclave and past the adobe home of Dollie Valdés Mondragón, one might just catch the delicious aroma of *chile verde con carne* wafting from off her trusty stove. The old Spanish recipe is one handed down from her beloved grandmother, Octaviana Martínez Valdés.

Chile Verde con Carne
(Green Chile Stew with Meat)

6 - 8 medium or large green chile pods (roasted and peeled, stems
and seeds removed, chopped)
(if chiles are small, use 10 - 12)
1 small lean pork roast
1 teaspoon salt
1/4 cup cooking oil
3 tablespoons flour
1 small onion, finely chopped
1 - 2 garlic cloves, finely chopped
1 can stewed tomatoes
1 pinch of pepper

Trim fat from meat and cook whole in medium saucepan with 6 - 8
cups of water. Add salt. Cook meat on low to medium heat for two hours
or until tender, adding water as needed. Allow meat to cool and shred
by hand or chop into small pieces. Reserve stock.

In dutch oven, heat cooking oil over medium heat. Add flour stirring
constantly until golden brown. Be careful not to burn! Add meat stock and
stir until mixture thickens. If too thick add water. Add remaining ingredients and meat. Continue to stir, adding water as needed. Simmer on low
heat for about 25 minutes to allow flavors to blend. Enjoy!

Recipe courtesy of Dollie Mondragón

In 1926, the lanky, mustachioed artist W. Herbert "Buck"
Dunton purchased a house on the west side of the plaza from
Indian trader Ralph Meyers. Dunton's love of the Southwest and
his passion to capture its vanishing glory on canvas brought him
to Taos in 1912. He painted what he felt most strongly about: preserving the unblemished tableau of "Old Taos" on canvas. He was
able to reproduce, with meticulous care, the details of Taoseños'
clothing, horses and equipment. This gave his works a remarkable
realism. Dunton's masterpiece, titled *Ginger*, portrait of a
swashbuckling cowboy friend, hangs today in the Harwood
Museum Gallery. Other works of note include *My Children*,
Partners of the Open Range and *The Bronco Busters*.

On the outskirts of the plaza, stretching east from the
corner of San Antonio and Camino de La Loma, sprawls a
row of Spanish adobe townhouses. Lacy, wrought-iron grills
enclose shadowy *portals*. These distinctive dwellings were constructed in the early 1800s in an attempt to create a second fortified bastion adjacent to the plaza. Here, on the corner in a rambling home with an old well, lived the legendary artist, Oscar
Edmund Berninghaus. He first came to Taos in 1899 on a commission for the Denver and Río Grande Railroad. On this junket,
Oscar boarded a narrow-gauge spur of the railroad called the
"Chile Line." The train crew strapped him to the brakeman's rail
on top of one of the freight cars so he could sketch the countryside better. Catching his first glimpse of Taos Mountain, he
was told that at its foot nestled one of the oldest villages in the
United States.

A St. Louis native, "Bernie," as he was nicknamed, was carried away by Taos with its Indian ponies, mountains and plains and especially the Pueblo Indians. By 1925, Berninghaus was widowed and moved to Taos permanently with his two children, Dorothy and Charles. Eschewing chaps, spurs and a cowboy hat, Bernie rose each day, put on a dark business suit, white shirt, tie and his usual Borsalino hat and went to work either in the mountains or in his studio. Passersby meeting him on the street would never have guessed he was an artist. His own evaluation was "People could mistake me for an undertaker."

Bernie's wonderful canvases include *Peace and Plenty* (St. Louis Art Museum), *The Rabbit Hunter* (Museum of Fine Arts, Santa Fe), and *The Overland Mail* (Philbrook Museum, Tulsa). Mabel Dodge Luhan, an old friend, once described the artist in these words: "Bernie's love for this valley in all its moods is painted in great sincerity and a close identification with its life. Few painters have studied the valley animals as deeply as he. He painted the pintos, the little Indian ponies, as well as handsome farm teams. As he lives deeply into his work, so his life comes poignantly out onto his canvases. Everybody feels "VIVA BERNIE!"

BILL HEMP

Governor Bent House and Museum
Mobs, Massacre and Martyrdom

This antique adobe structure was once the home of Charles Bent, an early trader, trapper and owner of wagon trains pulled by oxen over the Santa Fe Trail. He was a highly respected, much loved figure of the Old West. With the dynamics of Manifest Destiny put into full force by President James Knox Polk to expand to the width of the continent, Bent took office as the first civil governor soon after New Mexico became a United States possession in September of 1846.

Bent's early manhood was spent working for a fur company on the Missouri River. In the early 1830s he became interested in the Santa Fe trade and its fabulous profits. His first contact with New Mexico was through his experiences as a trader on the Santa Fe Trail. Later, Bent became associated with Cerain St. Vrain, a Frenchman of noble birth who moved to New Mexico from St. Louis. William Bent, Charles Bent and Cerain St. Vrain organized Bent, St. Vrain & Company, to facilitate trade with the Indians and other natives of New Mexico and southern Colorado. The partners established trading posts in Santa Fe, Taos, Bent's Fort, near present-day Las Animas, Colorado, Fort St. Vrain on the South Platte River and Adobe Walls in the Texas Panhandle.

The Bent caravans of mule and oxen hauled in merchandise from Missouri and in return received cash, buffalo hides and beaver skins. The company prospered, with numerous mountain men, French-Canadian and Native Americans working as their

traders. Kit Carson, at times, worked for Bent as a hunter and trapper. In fact, it is believed that Carson first came to New Mexico with one of the Bent caravans from Independence, Missouri.

Bent lived much of his mature life in northern New Mexico when it was part of Mexico. However, because he never became a Mexican citizen, Mexican officials often suspected that he might be an American spy—an allegation that was never proved. It was probably because of his reputation as a man of integrity in New Mexico and his esteem back in the states as a loyal American that Charles Bent was appointed New Mexico's first civil governor. On January 14, 1847, Bent, governor for less than five months, journeyed from Santa Fe to his hometown in Taos with the purpose of bringing his wife, Maria Ignacia Jaramillo, and their children to the territorial capital to reside.

New Mexico, which had been handed over to U.S. Army General Stephen W. Kearny by its Mexican Governor, Manual Armijo, was seething with discontent under the new U.S. government. On the outskirts of Taos, the Bent party encountered a group of Indians. They were emotionally charged on "Taos Lightning," a potent whiskey distilled in Arroyo Hondo and given to them by Mexican rebels in an effort to arouse them in their campaign to drive every American out of New Mexico. The Indians demanded that the governor release some of their men from the Taos jail. Bent told them the matter would have to be handled by the usual process of law, whereupon the angry crowd drifted slowly away.

Early in the morning of January 19, 1847, a large mob of native New Mexicans and Pueblo Indians had worked themselves into a state of frenzy. They gathered in the patio of the Bent house and, with a clamorous pounding on the door, demanded to see the governor. Bent's wife, Maria Ignacia, was the older sister of Josepha, Kit Carson's wife, who was visiting at the time. Maria pleaded with her husband to go out the back door and make a quick escape on one of the swift horses in the corral. But Bent refused and stayed behind to protect his family and placate the angry crowd storming the house. In his quiet, gentle way he attempted to calm the snarling, seething crowd.

He asked the boisterous mob, "What is it you want?"

They screamed, "We want your head, your *gringo* head. We want your scalp!"

Whispering to his wife, Bent told her to have the women inside dig a hole through the wall and escape to the adjoining house. With a large spoon and a fireplace poker, Mrs. Kit Carson and Mrs. Tom Boggs began chopping through the adobe wall. Soon the hole was big enough for the women and children to crawl through.

When he turned back to speak to the crowd, a bullet struck Bent squarely in the face. Making every effort to appease the blood-thirsty rebels, who were beyond reasoning, the governor lost his footing and an Indian leapt on top of him and ripped off his scalp with a long knife. Arrows struck him in the face and body. With every effort of his failing physical strength, Bent crawled slowly to the hole in the wall and the women pulled him through. His assailants were hot on his heels, and a final shot hit the courageous governor, who fell dead.

When peace had finally been restored to Taos, Maria Ignacia Bent returned to her home and found it totally demolished and looted. Very few of her former posses-sions remained intact. How-ever, her husband had given a handsome cherry-wood and leather chair to his friend, Kit Carson, who later gave it back as a gesture of sympathy. In the grim days to follow, those responsible for killing Governor Bent and the other Americans in Taos, were caught, brought to trial and hanged.

The Mexican and Indian revolutionaries' plan to rid New Mexico of Americans was doomed when Colonel Sterling Price set out to quash the uprising. With him were 480 men and Cerain St. Vrain with a contingent of Spanish and Anglo mountain men. After driving off 2,000 men at Santa Cruz, Price and his troops headed for Taos. They tramped through heavy snow and encountered the insurgents holed up in the massive adobe church of San Gerónimo at the Taos Pueblo. After a three-week revolt, the church lay in ruins. Captain Burgwin of the Union Army was killed in action, along with many Native Americans.

Since 1959, a museum and art gallery, run by Faye and Otto Noeding, has been housed in the Bent residence. On display inside are the spoon and poker used by the Bent family to dig through the thick adobe wall in an attempt to escape their attackers. The visitor can also view the governor's handsome chair and his trunk of hand-tooled buffalo hide. The trunk's front flap is emblazoned with the initials "C.B." That trunk accompanied Bent on many adventurous trips over the Santa Fe Trail. Today, a leisurely stroll through the Governor Bent House and Museum with its many

artifacts and heart-rending memorabilia truly opens "pages from the Historic West."

BILL HEWIT

"Long" John Dunn House
Gregarious Gambler and Taos Transport Tycoon

Back in the early part of this century visitors destined for Taos arrived at Servietta on the "Chile Line," a tiny railroad across the Río Grande that ran along the river bank from Alamosa to Santa Fe. The first person they encountered at the station was "Long" John Dunn. His task was to meet the train, which railroad men called "the two streaks of rust." The tracks were so loose that the weight of the engine pushing along at 18 miles an hour made them look like wriggling snakes. The train often arrived late because the engineer had spied a covey of quail and braked the train to bag a few. The obliging Dunn would then take the passengers bound for Taos in his dust-covered stage down through the Río Grande Gorge over the little bridge he owned. This provided him with a monopoly in toll charges plus fees for the journey from the train station to Taos.

"Long" John Dunn arrived in the Taos Valley from Texas in 1889 and immediately started a gaming business. A legend in his own time, Dunn was a man who never stopped defying authority. His action-packed career consisted of one hair-raising skirmish after another. He and his wife, Adelaide, resided in a small adobe at the intersection of Ranchitos Road and Ledoux Street. One day Dunn suspected that his heaping stockpile of firewood was rapidly diminishing through nefarious means. It was mid-winter and the house was quite cold. In an attempt to put a halt to the culprit's thievery, Dunn bored holes in some of the logs.

He stuffed them with blasting powder he had been asked to hide by some gold prospectors up in Twining Canyon, then plugged the holes with sawdust.

Called to Santa Fe for a political meeting, Dunn neglected to tell his dear wife what he had done. Ignorant of Dunn's protective measures, Adelaide placed an armful of logs in the cook stove to warm the house. Luckily, she then walked into the next room. One second later, there was a thunderous blast that knocked down one side of the house and blew the lovely lady onto Ledoux Street. Pregnant with her last child, John Jr., Adelaide and the baby fortunately were not injured in the frightful mishap.

Once settled in Taos, "Long" John Dunn put all of his energy into establishing a transportation business. He envisioned hotels, gambling houses and stables full of strong stagecoach horses. Hearing that a man named Meyers had constructed a bridge across the Río Grande at Taos Junction to serve passengers detraining at Servietta, Dunn was determined to buy it. He offered Meyers $4,000 for the span, but the owner held out for $15,000. Dunn then decided to go into the gambling business full swing. He acquired licenses for a game table in Gerson Gusdorf's popular hangout, the Don Fernando Hotel, and another at Mike Cunico's gambling house, "The Sleeping Boy," on South Pueblo Road.

After several months of successful winnings at the games, Dunn again approached Meyers asking if he was still keen on selling because he knew a particular party who just might want to purchase the wooden bridge over the Río Grande. Meyers surprised "Long" John by telling him he was willing to sell the span for $2,200 dollars. He would also give Dunn a $100 bonus if he would agree to serve as the go-between. Meyers walked off leaving Dunn with $15,000 in cash stuffed in his worn jeans, nearly fainting at the shocking change in price.

That night Dunn caught up with Meyers in the ornate lobby of the Don Fernando Hotel and presented him with a roll of greenbacks. After the crafty Meyers counted the money and scribbled out the bill of sale, it was time for the bridge owner to get his comeuppance. He asked, "Now, what is the name of the new owner?" The lanky Texan replied, "John Dunn," and added, "I thought it was such a bargain, I went and sold the bridge to myself."

As he had hoped, the toll bridge business proved lucrative, earning over two hundred and fifty dollars a day. Dunn's tariff was one dollar per person, fifty cents apiece for horses and cattle and twenty-five cents a head for sheep. On certain occasions, passengers arriving at Dunn's bridge would refuse to pay the steep toll fee. However,

their stubborn streak soon dissolved when they got a good look down the inside of Dunn's well-oiled shotgun barrel.

Not everything was sweetness and light for Dunn's passengers. During snowy winters the steep, rock-littered road that wound in and out of the Hondo Canyon to Taos was icy, slick and dangerous. As the creaking stage rolled up the narrow path, open on one side to the deep gorge carved over the centuries by the Río Hondo, highly nervous passengers fainted at the thought of tumbling down into the yawning abyss. During spring thaws, huge boulders often rolled down onto the roadway. "Long" John always carried a bundle of dynamite in the event the basalt chunks were too large to push out of the way.

With the advent of the automotive age, Dunn called a halt to his years in the saddle and the buckboard seat. He purchased one of the first Ford automobiles in Taos. Because of the treacherous, washboard mountain roads, John ordered brake lining by the hundred-foot roll.

Now, on top of all his other business interests, John applied for a mail route which included Taos Junction, Embudo Station and Servietta. Much of the parcel post involved paintings being sent in and out by prolific Taos pioneer artists like Joseph Sharp, E.I. Couse, Bert Phillips, Oscar Berninghaus and Ernest Blumenschein. Paintbrushes,

Belgian canvases and picture frames arrived from cities like New York, Boston and Chicago.

With his successes in gambling and transportation, "Long" John built a sprawling, ten-room house on Governor Bent Street, a block from the Taos Inn. The house, constructed of adobe but hard-plastered in Territorial style, was as strong as a fortress. Whether riding his stage, collecting bridge tolls, tending bar at his "Sample Room" on Taos Plaza, or standing behind his roulette wheel and gambling table stacked with silver, Dunn cut a famous figure. Six-feet-four from his boots up to his mustached face, he sported bright blue eyes that twinkled with devilment above his long nose. Standing in a crowd, he was impressive not only for his great height but also for his confident bearing. As an old pal once said of him, "Hell, you couldn't miss old John. He stood out among humans like a whore in church."

When "Long" John Dunn died quietly in May 1953, the newspaper, *El Crepúsculo*, ran an obituary written by doughBelly Price, gambler and rodeo-hand. It read: "There was just one John Dunn. The mold that made John, as I see it, reached the pinnacle of perfection and in that action they broke the mold. For he was truly a character, stage driver, cowboy and gambler . . . John lived through three phases of the West: the gun-fighting days, the cattle-working days, and the present-day modern West. That's a pretty complete coverage in anybody's language."

Today, driving down the rugged washboard road into the Hondo Canyon, one discovers that the old stagecoach trail is now traversed by oversized campers and four-wheel-drive Jeeps. Dunn's "Road Ranch" at the Río Grande has crumbled into oblivion. Passengers no longer come to Taos from Tres Piedras on the old "Chile Line." That was sold for scrap to Japan well before Pearl Harbor. But the John Dunn Bridge, although now constructed of shiny steel instead of local wood, still crosses the ever-flowing river. Walking across the short span, one might just hear the beat of horses' hooves pulling a mud-spattered stage and the gravelly voice of a tall Texan yelling "faster, faster" through his tobacco-stained, handlebar mustache.

Historic Taos Inn
Doc Martin, First and Fondest Physician in Town

This distinctive lodge straddles Pueblo Road. It basks in the glory of being the oldest hotel in town and the only one on the National and State Registers of Historic Places. The property on which the fashionable watering hole was built, appropriately on the site of the original town well, belonged to Dr. Thomas Paul Martin, the first and only physician in the entire county. When Doc Martin came to Taos in 1891, he purchased one of the largest houses in which to set up his practice. Dearly loved despite his irascibility and because of his deep concern for his fellow man, Doc was often required to hitch up his horse and black buggy, and later his "Tin Lizzie," and travel for miles through snow, sleet, biting wind and mud to deliver babies, attend fevers, heal gunshot wounds and set bones.

A glass alcove in the southwest corner of the inn's present-day dining room served as Doc Martin's delivery and surgery room as it afforded the best natural light. Many old-time *Taoseños* are affectionately known as "Martin's babies." Rose Martin, Doc's pretty younger sister, recalled that it was in this room that her husband, Bert Phillips, together with Ernest Blumenschein, came up with the idea to establish the Taos Society of Artists.

During the 1918 influenza epidemic at the Taos Pueblo, Martin, assisted by the artist Walter Ufer and his wife, worked day and night tending to the sick and dying. The country doctor who pronounced that "God's in charge of everything that happens in Taos" was hardly ever concerned whether or not his patients could pay their bills.

He appreciated a friendly act of barter in the form of a feathered chicken, a burlap bag full of potatoes or a haunch of venison in exchange for his visit. After Doc's death in 1936, his widow, Helen Martin, converted the residence and office into a small, intimate hotel. Earlier that year, the only hotel in town, the Don Fernando, had burned to the ground. Helen succeeded in making her dream come true by asking former patients of her late husband, who still had not paid their debts, to perform some of the labor necessary in the construction of the hotel. Sometime later an advertisement in the *Taos Review* read: "Your trip to Taos will be more pleasant, if you make our hotel, where every detail is typically Taos, your home. Rates $2.50 to $8.50. Every room with a bath."

Mrs. Hamilton Rapp of Santa Fe made the first reservation. Guests found the place decorated with Doc's famed collection of New Mexican handicrafts, which breathed the spirit of Taos in all its historic aspects. The cocktail room, the scene of the inaugural festivities, where Lowell Cheetham sang cowboy songs, was brightly painted with six murals by the local artist Ila McAfee Turner. It depicted prancing horses and pastoral scenes of the sprawling Taos Valley.

In 1948, Helen sold the hotel to Harold and Hilda Street, who owned "his and her" Rolls Royces. They made some renovations.

They renamed it the Taos Inn, added the neon thunderbird sign outside and installed the handsomely carved reception desk inside. The bell on top of the signboard in the front patio was once situated in the back courtyard. Harold rang it just about every day in order to fetch "August," his faithful Pueblo Indian caretaker.

The historic landmark served as host to such notables as Greta Garbo, who "wanted to be alone" in her courtyard *casita*, and Max Evans, the gregarious cowboy painter and writer of Western lore. Dee Strasberg (Daoma Winston), the author of numerous bestsellers, has been staying at the Taos Inn every year for two extended visits since 1951. She fondly recalls the lobby being filled with all sorts of Indian artifacts, saddles, rifles, and a big coffee urn perking in the glass alcove. She also fondly remembers the

barroom, with its lusty painting of a nude woman, being a nightly scene for fistfights and brawls, storytelling and singing. One ballad, written by Walt Sheldon, became a sort of theme song of Taos. It was sung by Ramon Hernandez and closed with this rollicking rhyme:

"You can be anything you want to be.
In a place called Fernando de Taos by the Río Grandee.
In Taos, New Mexico, there's no sexico.
Just intellexico."

From 1968 to 1981, the inn was taken over by Terry and Lavonne Moynihan. Everything ran smoothly until the early morning hours of October 1, 1978, when an electrical fire erupted in the kitchen. It burned through into the dining room and as far as the entryway. Thanks to the vigilant Taos Fire Department, which displays a rich collection of Taos painters' works all donated to their firehouse, the conflagration was quickly extinguished with hardly any damage to the guest rooms and no serious injuries. So grateful were the Moynihans that they purchased a gilded statue of Santa Bárbara, the patron saint of the hearth, in Mexico. Today, the lovely statue in flowing robes reposes in a glass case to

commemorate the event and invoke her revered protection. Since that time the Taos Inn has considered her their best possible insurance coverage.

After a tenure in the 1980s by a group of owners, the inn was purchased by Dr. Douglas Smith and his wife, Carolyn Haddoch, who have lovingly restored the hostelry to the status of a world-class tourist destination. The historic inn, which is well worthy of its motto, "An Adventure for Visitors, a Tradition for Locals," offers guests from Boston to Berlin forty commodious chambers featuring Southwest-style furnishings, hand-loomed Indian bedspreads and *kiva* fireplaces created by artisan Carmen Velarde.

With its romantic blue-and-white-tiled fountain and towering pine timbers that rise two and one-half stories to a stained-glass cupola in the cathedral ceiling above, the inn's lobby ranks as a favorite gathering place for *Taoseños* and travelers alike. Whether it's *aprés*-ski, following a "meet-the-artist" reception or a performance by flautist Robert Mirabel at the Taos Community Auditorium, The Adobe Bar at the south end of the lobby is a popular haunt for local artists, writers, politicians and townspeople. The bar's seating extends into the lobby, offering a cozy conversation pit and cocktail tables where guests can enjoy such celebrated margaritas as the "Cowboy Buddha" and "Hairy Dog."

"Doc Martin's," the inn's renowned restaurant, specializes in "High-Style Southwestern" cuisine, serving such delectable dinner entrees as corn-husk-smoked Churro lamb sirloin or lacquered duckling. On any evening, as one wends from the dining room to the lobby alive with conversation and music, one might just catch sight of a shadowy figure wearing a fedora hat smiling from the upstairs balcony. Don't be surprised—many *Taoseños* have seen Doc's ghost making his rounds, offering his services in exchange for the "Adobe Classic" margarita.

BILL HEMP

Nicolai Fechin House
The "Living Old Master" Carves a Niche in Taos

A tour through this creamy white adobe structure transports the visitor in Taos thousands of miles to Russia. Old-world ambiance is created by religious icons, handsome chests of warm-hued, hand-carved woods and massive fireplaces of splendidly balanced proportions. Nicolai Ivanovitch Fechin (1881-1955) was the consummate artist who designed and built this eastern-European-style home on Pueblo Road. He built it out of New Mexico mud over a seven-year period from 1927 to 1933. Fechin was a painter, sculptor, woodcarver and charcoal artist. What this Russian's eyes saw and his hands touched became a truly creative experience to be appreciated by others decades later.

Born in Kazan in the Tatarstan Region of Russia, Nicolai, at age four, fell dangerously ill. Faced with this crisis, his father, a talented woodcarver who built elaborate church altars, urgently requested that the priests of the parish hasten to the boy's bedside with an icon of the Madonna. When the priests passed the beloved icon over young Fechin, he regained consciousness and was soon healed. Asked if this story was true, the unpretentious Russian replied, "I had to fulfill my destiny as an artist."

In his mature years, Fechin would become a man of two continents. Half of his career was spent in Russia (1881-1923), where he studied at the Imperial Art Academy in Petrograd for seven years. At the conclusion of his apprenticeship, when given the opportunity to choose a teacher, he selected Ilya Repin, one of Russia's greatest artists, who praised Nicolai as "the most talented student to carry on after him."

Married to Alexandra "Tinka" Belkovitch in 1913, Nicolai began teaching art on his own. The long walks through bitter cold from his home to the schoolhouse brought on a bout with pneumonia and a touch of tuberculosis. Because he had sent his works to the Chicago Art Institute and the Carnegie Institute in Pittsburgh, which established his reputation in America, his students urged him to go there. In 1923, with his wife and young daughter, Eya, Fechin left Russia for New York. Residing there for four years, and making many new contacts and acquiring commissions, Nicolai became one of the four leading portrait painters in the city. Then, urged by British portrait artist John Young-Hunter to visit Taos, he decided to spend a summer there in 1926. Here, Fechin found in the Pueblo Indians a familiar echo of the Mongolian people he knew and loved in his mother country.

In 1927, having fallen in love with the landscape and the indigenous people, Fechin moved to Taos and set to work putting his endless supply of energy into building his house and pursuing his artistry. During his seven years in the valley, Nicolai painted many exceptional portraits and created wonderful wood carvings. Considering Taos his American home away from home, the meticulous "Living Old Master," with chiseled, high cheek bones and piercing eyes, labored around the clock over his paintings, charcoal drawings, sculptures and woodcarvings. Many called him the "Michelangelo of his time."

Utilizing his cherished collection of fine hand tools, English and German carving chisels, wood and leather mallets, sharpening stones, a hand grinding wheel, axes and a large adze, the indefatigable artist worked on his woodcarvings and sculptures. On the boards and beams of his beloved home, Fechin would finish with his adze, loving the texture and finish thus obtained.

As a youth he became incredibly adept with architectural construction, creating a blueprint drawing for a new chapel at the age of thirteen. As the years went by, he became even more proficient with the adze, obtaining a smooth, silky stroke that still delights woodworkers the world over. In his high-ceilinged studio behind the main house, Fechin painted in the early morning by natural light. When the light began to fail in the afternoon, he would then turn to his carvings and clay sculptures.

The visitor to the Fechin House enters through a glassed-in porch at the rear of the building, where Eya, the artist's petite daughter, is sometimes in attendance to offer a warm greeting. After her polite introduction to the history of the place, one proceeds into the dimly lit dining room, which contains a number of chests and sideboards carved by the artist in intricate, geometric designs that evoke his early years in Kazan. In the northeast corner of the room, known by Russian visitors as the "Beautiful" or "Red Corner," is an elaborately carved cabinet designed by Fechin. On it are displayed treasured icons. One belonged to Eya's grandfather; the Fechins brought it with them from the old country.

The spacious living room, entered through a richly carved swinging gate, is dominated by a beautifully balanced fireplace designed and built in the Russian style by Fechin. A wooden log carved into fascinating shapes rests on a beam above the hearth. A massive corbelled post supports the ceiling and is carved with whimsical Russian motifs that delight the eye. In the music room, a few steps down and dominated by a magnificent baby grand piano, one is charmed by an antique cabinet holding three miniature paintings by Fechin of his wife and daughter, along with an interesting collection of snuff bottles and figurines of ivory, jade and glass, given to the Fechin Institute by a friend of Nicolai's who accompanied him to Bali in 1938. The living room walls are hung with a gorgeous array of oriental art, scrolls and hangings Fechin acquired in exchange for his paintings. All are lighted by deep-set monastery windows inset with miniature round, leaded panes that have the sparkle of diamonds. In the master bedroom on the second floor, at the top of a beautifully carved, winding staircase, visitors are treated to changing exhibits, oftentimes including works by Fechin, such as *Alexandra with Coral Beads*, *Aspens*, and *Lady in Lavender*. Each one shows the bravura brushwork of the exuberant virtuoso.

The sun parlor, facing south, is splashed with New Mexican sunlight provided by mullioned windows on three sides. Displays of Fechin's work in clay and plaster are there along with *Bust of Alexandra* and a mounted head of *Eagle Feather Coming*, which are both cast in bronze. The connoisseur finds in all of Fechin's paintings an underlying structure of superb drawing along with a sense of lustrous color, daringly combined for the maximum of visual excitement. Still, each is rooted in natural appearance. Nicolai's portrait commissions over the years included such renowned subjects as Willa Cather, the writer; Lillian Gish, the actress; Mabel Dodge Luhan, the Taos hostess; Frank Waters, the author; and Duane Van Vechten, the artist.

After Fechin's seven-year labor of love and devotion to the construction of his Taos adobe, his wife, Tinka, demanded a divorce. Their agreement was that she would keep the house and he would stay in the studio. However, as time went by, the arrangement proved a failure. Broken-hearted at being torn from his cherished home, the "Old Master" moved to California with his daughter, Eya, who became a professional modern dancer. On the West Coast, he rented several studios and finally found an excellent space in Santa Monica. It was a studio measuring 40 by 40 feet and three stories high. There, accompanied by his pet dog, "Pepper," he worked from dawn till dusk, but at a slow pace, as this was the artist's natural bent.

In 1955, approaching the age of seventy-five, the Russian genius died quietly in his sleep. In the 1970s, his daughter took his ashes back to Kazan for burial. At the ceremony, attended by crowds of artists, friends and townspeople, an old acquaintance remarked, "Now we have him back. He is ours."

Today, the Fechin House and Studio have been designated New Mexico Cultural Sites and have been listed on the National Register of Historic Places since 1979. The Fechin Institute, formed in 1981, is a nonprofit educational and cultural foundation that uses the house for its activities. Each fall the annual Fechin Exhibition is held, as well as other shows of international scope. Recalling the Russian custom of respect on observing something beautiful, Nicolai oftentimes said, "When you find yourself in the presence of creativity . . . take off your hat!" That's exactly what each and every visitor should do on setting foot in the "Old Master's" beloved adobe in Taos.

BILL HEMI

Bert Phillips House and Studio
Pioneer Painter and Pueblo Indian Friend

It was just three decades after Kit Carson walked the furrowed paths of the frontier town that Bert Geer Phillips laid eyes on Taos and decided to stay and paint. The year was 1898, when he followed Ernest Blumenschein by several days into the valley and was immediately mesmerized by the brilliant light, the varied high desert, the painted-sky sunsets, and the presence of the Taos Indians. Phillips knew at once that he was going to stay in Taos but wanted other artists to join him. Months later, he wrote to Blumenschein who had returned to New York: "For heaven's sake, tell people what we have found. Send some artists out here. There's a lifetime of work for 20 men. Anyway, I'm lonesome."

Phillips' first studio in Taos was next door to the home of Governor Charles Bent, tragic victim of the Rebellion of 1847. It was a thrilling experience for him to sketch and paint the simple pueblo people. As he did, he learned to respect them and to become acquainted with them probably as well as any Anglo man could. The Taos Indians posed for him dressed in ceremonial costumes or simply wrapped in their multihued blankets in front of a *kiva* fire or by their sacred Blue Lake. As far as Bert was concerned, the Pueblo Indians were the first and only perfect models, as they could sit or stand absolutely motionless for hours.

It was Bert Phillips' intimate knowledge of the Indians and respect for their way of life, as well as his ability as an artist, that allowed him to put on canvas the very spirit of their day-to-day being. The Indians, in turn, held him in high respect and regarded his paintings with awe, considering them a kind of magic that even their medicine men could not accomplish. The Indians of Taos Pueblo were also grateful to Phillips for his assistance in gaining them perpetual rights to all the watershed above their pueblo.

Some years later, Bert Phillips moved to a larger studio at the corner of Pueblo Road and Martyrs Lane, named for those who died in the 1847 Rebellion. Here, he worked daily in a high-ceilinged room with a roof sloping upward and meeting the top edge of a huge north skylight window. On one wall stood a glass case containing baskets and pottery, beaded belts, moccasins and powder horns. In his early days, Phillips had become interested in Indian blankets, particularly finely woven Navajo blankets. As a result, the floor and chairs of his studio were covered with his very valuable collection. Looking into one corner of the studio, a visitor might see buckskin robes, leggings, quivers complete with bows and arrows and other artifacts. He would use these to dress up the models who posed for his paintings. In another corner, the Indians built a replica of one of their own rooms. It contained the typical beehive-shaped *kiva* fireplace, a low *banco* along one wall and an old buffalo robe on the floor.

While managing the Taos Indian Curio Shop and painting Indians in their pueblos, Bert experienced a severe problem with his eyes. He blamed it on the strain of painting by smoke-filled firelight. Reaching a point when he could paint only one hour a day, he was determined to find another occupation with which to support his wife, Rose, and two children, Ralph and Margaret. As luck would have it, the Taos Forest Reserve was taking applications for positions as forest rangers. Phillips took the Civil Service exam and was accepted for the job in 1907. His duties involved regulating the grazing of sheep, fighting fires and apprehending poachers. In 1908, when the Taos Forest and part of the Jemez Forest Reserves were combined into a national forest, Bert Phillips proposed that his boyhood hero, Kit Carson, be honored by naming the combined area Carson National Forest. Bert's proposal was enthusiastically approved.

Phillips then resigned from the Forest Service. He realized that the magical woodlands had begun to express spiritual messages and, with his eyes healed, knew it was time to go back to his easel and brushes at full throttle. He began work in earnest, painting Taos Indians and Hispanics, whom he most often portrayed showing dignified and stoic demeanors. Dubbed the "Taos Romantic," many of Phillips's oils are imbued with the attributes of solitude and silence. Others express such feelings as agony and ecstasy and chilvarous action. During this time in Taos, Bert established friendships with many Pueblo Indians. One in particular, a man called Tudl-Tur, or "Sunshine on the Elk," (Manuel Mondragón) became one of his frequent models. His initial canvases while in Taos were portraits of these Native Americans shown in a blunt, straightforward frontal position, which evoked a documentary spirit that recognizes the individuality of each sitter. One such painting, *Indian Warrior*, is a realistic portrait of Kit Carson's Apache scout, Nar-Ah-Kig-Coo-Ah-Tzuer, with his arrow case and bow bearing historical witness to his warrior past.

A high point of Phillips' career was his 1912 canvas, *The Water Carrier*, a soft-pastel image of a young pueblo woman. It was first shown in the Old Palace of the Governors in Santa Fe. His painting *Pueblo Indian Family* is a rare view of domestic life in which man, woman and child appear as a family, a subject very few Anglo artists dared to attempt. Bert's love of the great outdoors is evident in two of his master works. *Song of the Moonbow* features an Indian facing into the vastness of the night sky, his back to the viewer. *Indians Ice Fishing* shows colorfully draped hunters standing ready to spear their desired fish through a hole in the ice.

Later on, Phillips discovered that his landscapes of aspen trees growing in the mountains above Taos were proving popular with American art collectors. In his canvas *Aspen Forest* he created a marked contrast between the warm golden yellows of the aspen leaves with the cool blues of the distant mountains.

As Phillips was the first Anglo artist to live permanently in Taos, his life and the story of

the town's art colony have become legendary. For many years a brightly decorated float featuring a palette and a broken wagon wheel was drawn through the streets of town and around the Taos Plaza during the fiesta parade in summer. This float symbolized the creation of the town's artistic traditions by Bert Phillips and Ernest Blumenschein when they arrived in Taos and saw in it an ideal place to paint. This historic event was the catalyst to bring throngs of artists to the valley to express their own talents on canvas, paper, stone and textiles.

Bert Geer Phillips passed away in June 1956. His body was interred in Sierra Vista Cemetery next to that of his lovely wife, Rose. Phillips had converted to the Catholic faith in his latter days, and a Requiem Mass was said for him in Our Lady of Guadalupe Church. At the entrance to the candle-lit sanctuary stood a silent group of Taos Pueblo Indians, lined up to play tribute to the painter. This gesture was a fitting finale to the life and career so inspired by pueblo culture.

PILL HENY

Stables Art Center
The Unsolved Mystery of Arthur Rochford Manby

This house in the heart of Taos on Pueblo Road, now the Stables Art Center, was once the residence of Arthur Rochford Manby, who came from an aristocratic British family. His great-grandfather, Dr. Edward Manby, was a surgeon in the Royal Navy and served as an aide to Captain James Cook during the discovery of Australia in 1775. Manby came to New Mexico in the early 1880s seeking to take advantage of the vast opportunities available in ranching, farming and mining. He was well educated, having trained as an architect in Belfast, Ireland, and was skilled in mineralogy and oil painting as well.

By the time he set foot in Taos in 1883, Manby entertained ambitions to amass a large fortune in real estate. Once established in town, he purchased seven parcels of property, approximately 23 acres, just north of Kit Carson's home and east of the main road to Taos Pueblo. As an architect of note, Manby promptly launched into designing and building an expansive Spanish-style hacienda. It comprised nineteen rooms arranged in a square with three wings and stables. The compound was entirely surrounded by outer adobe walls.

Finally completed in 1907, the house boasted rough plank floors, spruce rafters and walls plastered with *tierra blanca*. Manby landscaped the hacienda in the English style with a flagstone courtyard inset with thick grass, a middle patio with a well that still exists today, and a third patio next to the stables.

What is now Kit Carson Park was designed as an English garden with groves of elm, linden and locust trees, curving walkways and sunken pools. Hollyhocks, poppies and roses bordered the well-kept lawns. The north side of the house, from which Manby could enjoy the view of Taos Mountain, was framed with over two hundred lilac bushes. He also instructed his Indian gardeners to plant hundreds of cottonwood seedlings along Pueblo Road at the front of the hacienda. Manby was careful to select only male trees, which do not shed. When Bert Phillips, the artist who lived across the way, put in female cottonwoods, which drop copious fluffs that permeate the air, Manby flew into a rage.

The interior of the hacienda was furnished with English antiques of mahogany and walnut. It contained fine oil paintings, including a Van Dyck, which later secured the future of the house.

In December 1919, Mabel Dodge Sterne arrived by stage in Taos. Her first objective was to rent the "largest and most attractive house in town." Although she wasn't particularly impressed with the Manby mansion, which had slowly deteriorated, she decided to pay the monthly rent of $75. The Englishman consequently was obliged to move out of the main quarters and live in the smaller west wing. When Mabel departed to build her own home on Morada Lane with the help of her lover, Tony Luhan, the reclusive Englishman went to seed and the property steadily fell into disrepair.

For the last twenty years of his life in Taos, the infamous Manby made a business of selling bogus quitclaim deeds, negotiating numerous property deed manipulations and maneuvering superstitious tenants to return the properties that he had previously sold them. Over the years he created a growing army of enemies for his unscrupulous, heavy-handed tactics. He bilked the unwary and gullible by inflating the prospects of gold mining ventures. In short, Mr. Manby was disliked with a passion.

On Thursday, July 4, 1929, an awful event occurred. Arthur Rochford Manby was found dead in his hacienda. His body was said to be in a mutilated condition with the head severed from the torso. The story goes that there

were two adjacent bedrooms in the front of the house. Manby's head was found by the police in one, and his bludgeoned body was discovered in the other. Thus began "the greatest unsolved mystery of the Southwest." Was it Manby's decapitated body in the house? Or was it someone he had murdered and substituted for himself to make a quick escape from his enemies? To further complicate the

case, it seems that several years later, Taos artist Joseph H. Sharp and his wife, strolling across a sunny *piazza* in Florence, Italy, suddenly caught sight of the familiar figure of A. R. Manby, wearing his usual knickers and with his same bow-legged walk. When the elusive landowner spotted the Sharps, he hastily ducked into a shop and vanished forever from sight. The bizarre riddle of the demise of Arthur Rochford Manby has never been solved to this very day.

Years later, the spacious property passed to Dr. Victor Thorne, a wealthy New York art collector who had purchased the Van Dyck painting from Manby some time before. Holding a second mortgage on the house, Thorne, with hopes of making the hacienda a summer getaway for his family, dispatched an associate, Miss Helen Williams, to Taos to check out the condition of the property. She telegraphed Thorne that the house was beyond repair, but he insisted she go ahead with the rebuilding anyway. Williams hired a master craftsman who transformed the place between the years 1937 and 1940. Unfortunately, Dr. Thorne never made it to his refurbished adobe. He died suddenly in New York city, without even leaving a will.

Miss Williams, who now had title to the place, renamed it Thorne House and opened the doors as a community center. In later years, her ambition to see the hacienda remain open to serve the public found a perfect fulfillment. Painter Emil Bisttram had a long-time dream to create a museum and gallery for the artists of Taos. As a result of the Williams-Bisttram partnership, what is now known as the Taos Art Association (TAA) was founded.

In 1952, the TAA bought the Thorne House property, the stables and three acres to the east. During the decade that followed, the main building served as the repository of the newly founded Millicent Rogers Museum. Finally, in 1972, the TAA decided to move the art gallery from the stables to the front of Thorne House after the Millicent Rogers Museum was established north of town.

Just behind what is now called the Stables Art Center stands the Taos Community Auditorium, which presents a galaxy of eclectic entertainment including drama, dance, classical music, Native American talent, children's plays and motion-picture classics. The memorable cornerstone laying was held on September 18, 1971, with musical entertainment provided by *Los Taoseños*, featuring the ever-popular Hattie Trujillo strumming out rhythms on her mandolin accompanied by the talented Nat Flores on the guitar.

Today, the Stables Art Center thrives as the vibrant heart of the community, providing a sparkling showcase for artists of Taos and the surrounding valley. Supported by over 900 paid members in an arts-oriented town of 4,500, the TAA is proud of the fact that it is the oldest community art organization in New Mexico and one of the most respected in the vast Southwest.

Although Arthur Rochford Manby's bizarre murder has never been solved, it seems likely that the Englishman's swindling led to his undoing. Manby's gravestone in Kit Carson Cemetery is engraved with these words: "He planted the trees in this park and on Pueblo Road." But he did it with the help of Taos Pueblo Indian Tony Luhan!

Van Vechten-Lineberry Taos Art Museum
Myriad of Masterpieces at El Rancho de la Mariposa

Since its public opening in December 1994, swarms of art lovers have descended upon a ten-acre estate hidden behind pink adobe walls and shaded by 756 towering, 60-year-old blue spruce and assorted other trees near the entrance to Taos Pueblo. The crown jewel of the enchanting compound, named by its owners El Rancho de la Mariposa, is the Van Vechten-Lineberry Taos Art Museum, built by Edwin C. and Novella Lineberry in memory of Edwin's first wife, the late artist Duane Van Vechten, and as a memorial to the art and artists of Taos. Because of his love for the arts, Edwin Lineberry wanted to create a central location in which to preserve and display works by members of the Taos Society of Artists, many of whom were personal friends and guests in his home. These talented individuals became recognized worldwide for their oil paintings, watercolors and etchings.

Complete with Indian coral stucco and architectural details that match the original 1929 studio, the museum boasts approximately 20,000 square feet of display area and state-of-the-art security, lighting and climate control systems. Duane Van Vechten's studio, which served as the Lineberry home until the main house was constructed in 1938, is now the front entrance to the imposing complex. Once inside, the visitor is welcomed by a cathedral-ceilinged studio featuring two *kiva* fireplaces and an ornate balcony with hand-carved corbels. One's eyes are quickly attracted to a gaming table with a solid brass roulette wheel purchased by

Lineberry from the old Taos trader and stage driver "Long" John Dunn. A photograph of Duane Van Vechten beckons guests to enter the magnificent museum dedicated to her memory.

In 1935, Edwin Lineberry met Duane Van Vechten. Miss Van Vechten had spent summers in Taos with her mother building the old studio, which took them three years to construct. She studied at the Chicago Art Institute, where she won honors for her work. Time was also spent under the instruction of Ivan Lorraine Albright, who painted *The Picture of Dorian Gray* that turned from handsome to hideous in the Hollywood film based on the Oscar Wilde novel. Van Vechten also showed her works at the New Mexico Museum of Art and worked with many of the Taos founders.

During her residence in New Mexico, Van Vechten painted still-lifes, landscapes and her favorite subject, butterflies, hence the name El Rancho de la Mariposa and the logotype for the Museum. Although Duane's paintings were rarely sold (because of the artist's desire to keep them herself), she was a versatile artisan working in a variety of media, especially watercolors. Her last painting titled *Gladiolus*, which she was working on before her death in 1977, stands on an easel in the studio entrance. The muted pastel shades of pink and lavender blossoms make for a particularly fitting memorial to a prolific painter.

Novella Lineberry was the driving force behind the metamorphosis that turned El Rancho de la Mariposa into a stunning, state-of-the-art facility. She watched over the small architectural and electronic details, such as the shape of the corbels to support the roof beams and the selection of music for the sound system. "There's not a museum anywhere that has all the Taos founders," she said in an interview with the *Taos News*, "The idea is to keep the art of Taos in Taos, where, if you're visiting and want to see Taos artists, you'll be able to do that." Edwin Lineberry then added, "I think people who come to Taos would like to see a collection of all the Taos founders."

Once the visitor enters the vast museum gallery area, the Lineberrys' promise of Taos founders' treasures comes true. Breathtaking works by the six original charter members of the Taos Society of Artists—Joseph H. Sharp, Ernest L. Blumenschein, Bert Geer Phillips, Oscar E. Berninghaus, E. Irving Couse and W. Herbert Dunton—dominate the walls. Oil paintings, watercolors and etchings of the five other artists who were made active members later—Walter Ufer, Victor Higgins, Kenneth Adams, Catherine Critcher (the only woman ever elected to the society) and E. Martin Hennings—are also represented in the eclectic collection amassed by the Lineberrys over the years. Other artists represented include Julius Rolshoven, Robert Henri, John Sloan, Randall Davey and B.J.O. Norfeldt.

In the gallery devoted to the art of Duane Van Vechten, the visitor can admire *Portrait of Genevieve*, *Paper Poppies*, *Head Life of Miss Benedict* and *China Cat*, for which she won honors at the Chicago Art Institute, and *Yellow Drapery*, a stunning work that has three-dimensional characteristics.

Some of the highlights of the Taos founders' collection include a magnificent painting of a Taos Indian in full headdress titled *Portrait of John Reyna,* by W. Herbert "Buck" Dunton, *Portrait of The Hunter* by Catherine Critcher, a voluptuous oil by Victor Higgins titled *Indian Nude*, *The Cottonwoods* by E. Martin Hennings and *Crossing the Arroyo* by Oscar E. Berninghaus. Other oils to be admired include *Taos Indian Holding Horse in Mountains* by Walter Ufer, *Taos Landscape* by Ernest Blumenschein and *Warbonnet Shadows* by Bert Geer Phillips. The latter, featuring a Taos Pueblo Indian by firelight, is a most extraordinary portrait of a Native American. Also to be seen in the collection are works by later Taos artists such as the Russian painter Leon Gaspard, Andrew Dasburg, Dorothy Brett and many others. Edwin Lineberry and wife Duane together built and operated the Kachina Lodge next door to the estate. Duane designed the unique Southwestern interiors of the lodge as well as the wooden totem pole in the center of the circular Kiva Coffee Shop. The intricate carvings, Novella Lineberry explained, are meant to represent "Bird, Beast, Man and Infinity." A painting showing the totem pole in progress hangs in the studio entrance of the museum.

With its myriad of masterpieces by the legendary Taos founders, the Van Vechten-Lineberry Taos Art Museum seems destined to become a major landmark in the years to come. Visitors from all over the world will journey to the high country of northern New Mexico to see if the sky is as turquoise blue as the talented Taos Society of Artists have painted it. They certainly won't be disappointed by the magnificence that awaits them behind the pine-shaded pink adobe walls of El Rancho de la Mariposa.

BILL HEMP

San Gerónimo de Taos Pueblo
Multi-tiered Adobe, Mystical Mountain, Sacred Blue Lake

According to legend, Taos Pueblo was founded over a thousand years ago by a great chief who, tracking an eagle, led his people up a swift moving stream to the base of the mountain. The majestic bird then let fall two plumes, one landing on each side of the Río Pueblo. Here the people constructed their new homes out of adobe. The two main structures are *Hlauma* (north), five stories high and eleven rooms wide, and *Huakwima* (south), also five stories high. Both structures are of similar age. They are believed to be the oldest continuously inhabited communities and the largest existing multistoried pueblos in the United States.

San Gerónimo de Taos Pueblo—called *Tua-Tah* by its Tiwa speaking people—was most likely completed between 1350 and 1450 A.D.—long before Christopher Columbus landed in the Americas. Spanish conquistadores, led by Captain Hernando de Alvarado, scouting for the famed explorer Francisco Vasquez de Coronado, found their way into the Taos Valley in 1540 and discovered the glistening, straw-speckled adobe pueblo, which they believed to be one of the fabled "Golden Cities of Cibola." The two structures, with their recessed rooftops, appeared then much as they do today. The buildings are built entirely of mud-mortar, made of clay-bearing soil, straw and water. They are then plastered over, making them seem to grow out of the earth.

Taos Pueblo is unquestionably the most beautiful of New Mexico's pueblos in its setting against the green, mountainous backdrop under a blue dome of sky filled with masses of billowing cumulus clouds. The two "apartment houses" hold within their foot-thick walls a way of life little changed by the passage of time.

A combination fortress and apartment building, the pueblo is actually a honeycomb of private homes, built side by side and in layers, with common walls and connecting doorways. In days of old, the pueblo had no doors or windows. Entry was gained only from the top as a protection against marauding Apache and Comanche Indians. The roofs of the pueblo are supported by *vigas*, large pine timbers hauled down from distant forests. *Latillas*, smaller poles of aspen or pine, are placed side by side on top of the *vigas*, then covered with packed dirt. In 1776, Fray Dominguez reported that the north and south pueblos were connected by a wall with towers where the walls met the Río Pueblo. By the 1500s, blocks of rooms were reserved for visiting traders of the Apache, Comanche and Kiowa tribes.

The Taos Pueblo was unique in relations with other Indian groups. Because of its location close to the plains, pueblo residents traded with the Apache and Comanche regularly. The village served as a point of contact between Pueblo and Plains tribes. "Trapper fairs" were held and everyone came—French and American trappers, mountain men, Spaniards, *Comancheros* and Indians from many tribes. There was a veritable cornucopia of earthly riches available for trade or barter. There were multicolored abalone shells from the Pacific, magnificent macaws from Central America, woolly warm buffalo robes from the plains, thick blankets woven of rabbit fur, copper bells and glossy blue-green turquoise.

Mystical Taos Mountain, a monument of nature's sculpture and a sacred symbol to the Pueblo Indians, presides over the pueblo. Its snowcapped peak reaches an altitude of over 12,000 feet. High within its contours and nestled in a crater lies the sacred Blue Lake, seen only by Native Americans. The lake was returned to Taos Pueblo by the U.S. government in 1970. The crystal-clear waters of the Río Pueblo, or Red Willow Creek, as it is also called, flow from the Blue Lake watershed. It still serves as the primary source of fresh water for the inhabitants. There is no electricity in the historic section of Taos Pueblo.

The sun-drenched, spacious plaza is still used for dancing, baking bread and drying food. Here one can drink in the pueblo's panorama. Native Americans are wrapped in blankets of blazing colors or shawls of white. They look out from terraces over the countryside as they go about their daily duties in one of the most spectacular settings anywhere. *Kiva* ladders lead to upper levels and cast multiringed shadows against golden ramparts pierced by hand-hewn *vigas*. Willow trees create lacy shadows on the stream bed. Adobe walls are punctuated by doors and windows painted Taos blue, a color believed to ward off evil spirits. Outside, in the outdoor, dome-shaped ovens called *hornos*, the women bake their bread just as their ancestors did centuries ago. Curio shops are scattered about the plaza. They offer visitors a galaxy of gorgeous hand-crafted items created by pueblo artisans. There are mica-flecked pots, first developed between 1550 and 1600 A.D., silver bracelets, necklaces of turquoise and rainbows of semiprecious stones, butter-soft moccasins and drums of timeless designs.

During particular feast days, the Taos Pueblo Indians, whose way of life emphasizes the importance of religious traditions, hold ceremonial dances and processions in the well-trodden plaza compound. Turtle Dances are held on January 1 and Buffalo or Deer Dances on January 6. Foot Races and Corn Dances may be seen on the Feast of Santa Cruz, May 3. One can witness Corn Dances on the Feast of San Antonio, June 13, and the Feast of San Juan, June 24.

On the second weekend in July, Indian tribes from across the nation converge on the valley for the annual Taos powwow. This is a long-awaited event at which Native Americans delight themselves and thousands of onlookers by parading and dancing in their intricately sewn costumes, which are often beaded and made with fringed buckskin. Some dancers carry shields of buffalo skins and are crowned by elaborate headdresses of eagle and macaw feathers.

On July 25 and 26, the Feast of Santiago and Santa Ana, Pueblo Indian women are fitted out in costumes they've been working on all year long. Their feet are shod in wide, folded white buckskin boots, unique to the pueblo. The women nobly perform their traditional Corn Dances.

On September 29 and 30, the feast of the pueblo's patron saint, San Gerónimo, visitors from every corner of the world witness the famous foot races, polished pole climbings and the Sunset Dances, a spectacle not to be missed.

On Christmas Eve the pueblo holds a procession through the plaza amid blazing bonfires. On Christmas Day Deer Dances, or *Matachines,* are performed.

Visitors are welcome at the pueblo, located just three miles north of Taos Plaza. At the entrance stands the little whitewashed adobe chapel of San Gerónimo de Taos, a Catholic mission church completed in 1850. The original edifice, built in 1619, was destroyed during the war with Mexico by the U.S. Army in 1847. The ruined sanctuary now serves as a cemetery for Taos Indians. With a land base of over 95,000 acres, much of Taos Pueblo Reservation is cultivated and used for grazing horses and a herd of American bison. It has a population of over 1,750 residents. Part of the pueblo's economy is built on tourist trade, arts, crafts and food concessions. Today, a great majority of Taos tribal members choose to stay on pueblo land, thus acknowledging their important cultural heritage. It comes as no surprise that in 1975 Taos Pueblo was declared a National Historic Landmark and in 1992 was enlisted in the United Nations World Heritage Society as one of the most significant cultural landmarks in the world. It is the only living community to be honored by this recognition.

Millicent Rogers Museum

Repository of an Avid Collector's Treasures and Talents

The wealthy, socialite granddaughter of Henry Huttleston Rogers, one of the founders of Standard Oil with John D. Rockefeller, was Millicent Rogers. Her blonde, statuesque beauty many times graced the covers of fashion magazines, Harper's Bazaar and Vogue. She found Taos in 1947. Throughout her life, the chic Millicent, born in 1902, moved in elite social and cultural circles in America and Europe. On both continents, whether living on large estates or in rented castles, she was continuously designing homes and gardens, clothing and jewelry. When she danced with the Prince of Wales during his American tour in the 1920s, Millicent made a smashing impression with her wide-set eyes and her arched eyebrows. Rogers expressed the Taos landscape and local cultures in "Turtlewalk," the lovely adobe home she built on Ranchitos Road, the native clothes she wore and the exquisite art she avidly collected.

Blessed with a keen intellect, a restless energy and a passionate artistic and literary sense, Millicent began collecting Native American jewelry, textiles, baskets and pottery as well as Kachina dolls, rugs, blankets and Spanish art. These included Colonial furniture, *santo* carvings, unique *Doña Sebastian* death carts and Río Grande weavings. Her priceless collection forms the nucleus of the magnificent museum that bears her name today. Founded in 1953, the year Rogers died, the museum was first housed in artist Mabel Degan's home on Ledoux Street, then in the Stables Gallery.

Its present site is the former one-story adobe residence of Claude and Elizabeth Anderson. Named "Dow Hill," the site is high on the windswept mesa northwest of Taos. Here, the unsuspecting visitor is quickly swept up in the spectacle of walls and exhibit cases glowing with an amazing array of pottery, sculpture, jewelry, wood carvings and architectural artifacts.

Since 1984, the museum has been home to the largest collection of San Ildefonso Pueblo pottery created by the Martínez family: Maria, her husband, Julian, her son, Popovi Da and Grandson, Tony Da. Almost alone in the Indian art world, this assemblage of exquisitely painted black-on-black pottery was made and preserved by its makers—the most important family of pueblo potters in the Southwest. Responsible for the revival of the San Ildefonso pottery tradition, Julian painted matte-finish designs with a red clay slip on the highly polished vessels formed by Maria. Smothering during the firing process produced the desirable black-on-black effect. After their marriage in 1904, the couple traveled to St. Louis to demonstrate pottery making at the Louisiana Purchase Centennial Exposition held there.

One of the modern *objets d'art* that bedazzles the eye at the Rogers Museum is *Seated Lady*, a bronze sculpture created in 1977 by R.C. Gorman, the Navajo artist. The statue greets guests in the leafy inner courtyard. Other marvelous treasures include a black-on-black jar with an image of an antelope, circa 1919. It is one of the earliest vessels made by Maria and Julian. There is a Buffalo Kachina, circa 1875, a superb example of Zuni religious art, which was acquired by the well-traveled Rogers from a trader at the Zuni Pueblo in the late 1940s. There are strings of turquoise and white shell beads called *heishi*, used by all the pueblo peoples since prehistoric times and Anasazi black-on-white pottery, including a Tularosa jar with swirls and curlicues, circa 1100-1250 A.D. Such jars were used for storing water and were produced in the Four Corners area, which includes Chaco Canyon, Mesa Verde, Kayenta, and the Río Grande Valley.

Other visual treats in store are Tom Burnside's Shop, the pride of a Navajo silversmith who worked in the 1940s. It holds a plethora of his tools: anvils, torches, hammers, crucibles, ingot molds, grindstones, files, chisels and tongs. In the Gallery of Hispanic Religious and Domestic Art, one is quickly attracted to a Hispanic loom, built circa 1830 and acquired from the Montaño Family of El Prado and Arroyo Seco. A low-beamed *zambullo* door, circa 1870, typical of early northern New Mexico construction—its name is derived from the Spanish verb, *zambullir*, "to duck one's head"—serves as the entryway to the gallery of religious art. Here are displayed a unique body of ecclesiastical icons: carved *bultos* and *retablos*, painted portraits of saints and other sacred personages.

Particularly noteworthy is a door carved by Patrocino Barela, one of Taos' most important Hispanic artists of the 20th century, a wood sculptor unique in his art. The meticulously carved panels portray Biblical scenes, three of which are part of the Christmas Pageant—the three kings, the killing of male children by Herod's order and the flight into Egypt by the Holy Family. In the gallery devoted to the artistry of Millicent Rogers, a number of showcases display the chic, stunning jewelry she designed while living in the Taos Valley. Her fabulous eye for color and texture and a daring knack for juxtaposition led her to produce more than three hundred jewelry designs, including her gorgeous *Fan Necklace of Sheet Silver*, *Shimmering Moon* earrings, the *Medicine Flower Bola*, *Gerónimo's Cross* and other precious items studded with huge turquoise stones.

Expanding her creative horizons to automobiles, Millicent completely changed the silhouette of her French-made 1939 Delage sports car, considered a very fast vehicle for its time. She added a single, elegant fin running down the back, lengthened the rear fenders and lowered the roof, resulting in an extremely rakish look for the gun-metal gray automobile. She drove it for years until she sold it to a collector. Later, in New York she upgraded a Checker Cab by having it upholstered in tiger skin and used it as her private limousine.

After three brief marriages—to Count Ludwig Salm Von Hoogstraeten, a former Austrian cavalryman; Arturo Peralta-Ramos, an Argentine sportsman; and Ronald Balcom, a Wall Street broker, Millicent Rogers carved out a new career. She had the vision and conviction to collect and preserve the precious but rapidly vanishing arts of Native Americans and Spanish Colonialists. European fashion critics considered her to be one of a very few select American women who illustrated a great "sense of style." Going beyond the acquisition of artifacts and creating exquisite jewelry, Millicent Rogers became enveloped in the Native American world view. She wrote about the effect of Taos Mountain on her:

"I felt that I was part of the Earth
I felt the sun on my surface and the rain
I felt the Stars and the growth of the Moon
Under me Rivers ran
And against me were the tides
The waters of rain sank into me
I thought if I stretched out my hands

They would be earth and green would grow from them
And I knew that there was no reason to be lonely
That one was everything."

The Millicent Rogers Museum, located above El Prado on Museum Road, serves today as a living memorial to a stunning woman with unassailable taste and a tradition for preserving the treasures of the indigenous peoples of New Mexico.

(Drawing of Millicent Rogers adapted from a photograph by Dahl-Wolfe for Harper's Bazaar, 1946.)

Turley's Mill
Taos Lightning, Trappers and Turbulence

Deep down inside the Río Hondo Valley north of Taos, the history buff happens upon the half-hidden ruins of one of the first industrial enterprises west of the Mississippi, one that was tightly entangled in the early era of the Americanization of the Southwest. This was Turley's Mill, which produced a "mountain dew" originally known as *aguardente* and later affectionately called "Taos Lightning." The wheat-based whiskey, flavored with such potent ingredients as tobacco, gunpowder and pepper, was said to seize imbibers with a fiendish desire to kill someone.

Simeon Turley was born in the same county in Kentucky as Kit Carson and was a longtime friend of Carson. In 1830, Turley discovered a clear mountain stream along the old Kiowa Indian Trail. This trail, also known as the Taos Trapper's Trail, passed near the ancient Spanish village of Arroyo Hondo (deep ditch). Turley saw the possibilities of doing business in the area, which at that time was the granary and bread basket of the West, and decided to make his living there. Having the benefit of experience in a number of trades, including those of merchant, farmer, livestock producer, miller and distiller, he asked himself, "Why not make the most of it?" Purchasing over 200 acres of valley land, he dug irrigation ditches, planted wheat, raised hogs and put in a water wheel and a stone mill to grind the grain. Later, he started a distillery with the fast-flowing stream running right through it. Turley's operation was soon to become famous all over the frontier, as Taos, at the time, was a place of merriment and rest for the weary traveler, mountain man, trader and explorer.

Simeon Turley's distillery used all the surplus grains grown in the Taos Valley in the making of its product. This provided an enormous source of revenue for the ranchers in the area. "Taos Lightning," the hard drink of the Southwest, was taken out of New Mexico by Charles Autobees, one of Turley's employees. This extended his trade in furs, buffalo hides, produce and merchandise to cover the liquor market. French fur trappers and mountain men bartered beaver pelts, tanned skins and other harvests of western forests and streams for the intoxicating brew. Of great importance was the annual rendezvous of the traders, trappers and Indians. Turley's whiskey seemed always in great demand. Then, in 1842 the U.S. government began to enforce a ban on the exportation of whiskey to the Indians, but the Turley operations in New Mexico continued to thrive.

The mountain man's lexicon included a slew of nicknames for Turley's potent whiskey, such as Popskull, Panther Milk, Tarantula Juice and Tanglefoot. The cowboys in the valley were heard to say about the potency of the beverage, "Three drinks of it will actually make you save your drowning mother-in-law." The *Coureurs de Bois*, or voyager type of trappers, flourished in the early 1800s when John Jacob Astor was rising to power in the fur trade. In 1831, many of them were working for American fur companies. They drifted down from Canada to partake of the profits from overstocked Rocky Mountain streams.

The Taos rendezvous was an event the trappers looked forward to every year. It was a debauch with plenty of whiskey. Finally, there would be trade goods, on which the trapper would have to focus his attention, for he would need to outfit himself for the coming year with traps, blankets, powder, lead and flints. In those young years, the mountain men would converge on the Plaza of Don Fernando de Taos and look over the wagons that had just arrived over the Santa Fe Trail, opened by William Becknell, whose bold mule-train caravan blazed the route in 1821. There, they would watch the men buy hardware and the women purchase silk slippers imported from Paris, France. Crowds witnessed men outfitting for the mountains, swapping mules, replacing saddles, buying traps, packing dried meat, sharpening their hunting knives and cleaning their weapons. The trappers were men like old Bill Williams, Ewing Young, Antoine Robidoux, Cerain St. Vrain, Jean Jeantet, Abraham Ledoux and Carlos Beaubien. They were warmly clad and pursued their hunting when the weather permitted, trapping beaver in the streams before they froze. When the winter blasts swept down from the north and snow piled up around their quarters, they stayed indoors, made moccasins, cleaned equipment and cooked buffalo steaks and "son-of-a-bitch stew," enriched with the brains of steers.

Meanwhile, as Turley's enterprise in Taos Valley flourished, there was the threat of violence by the local Mexicans and Pueblo Indians, angered at having the whites take over their land. The American Territorial Governor, Charles Bent, decided to make a trip home to Taos even though he had been warned that trouble was brewing. After the drunken mob of insurgents had invaded his home and scalped and murdered him before the terrified eyes of his loved ones, the rebellion spread rapidly to Arroyo Hondo, only 12 miles to the north of Taos.

Simeon Turley, advised of the grim news of what had happened in Taos, felt confident that he would be spared, because he was well liked by his employees and neighbors. At the suggestion of his eight Anglo helpers, he agreed to close the gates and stand ready to defend the mill. It wasn't long afterwards that a bloodthirsty gang of 500 Mexicans and Pueblo Indians came upon the scene. They shouted out to Turley that if he would surrender his property and the workers with him, they would let him go free. Stubborn and bull-headed, as was his nature, the distiller refused, and the bloody battle of Turley's Mill began in earnest.

By nightfall, the insurrectionists, using not only muzzle-loading rifles but bows and arrows, lances, knives and clubs as well, had taken the stables. Still, Turley and his men held the mill with all the courage they could possibly muster. The skirmish renewed in the morning, with reinforcements for the insurgents coming from Taos and distant villages. In a final desperate attempt to break through the thick, rock-strong bastions of the mill, the rebels began to burn the defenders out. After extinguishing a rash of minor fires, Turley and his men could no longer control the conflagration. At this point it was every man for himself.

To save his skin, the frightened Turley managed to escape under the cover of black, billowing smoke out of a back door of the mill. Heading east toward the Sangre de Cristo Mountains, he encountered a Mexican man, a friend of many years' standing. Intent on eluding the dreaded mob, Turley offered his valuable timepiece in exchange for the man's horse. The Mexican advised him to head out immediately for a certain abandoned ranch and hide. He promised to deliver a fast horse and a basket of food to him after dark. Unfortunately, Simeon followed the instructions to the letter. With the distiller gone, his former friend, now turned traitor, galloped back to the still-burning mill where the insurgents were looting the house, mill and stables of everything they could lay their hands on. The Mexican told the mob of Turley's hiding place. Then, with shrill screams of vengeance, the

bloodthirsty crowd of bandits raced to the ranch, seized Turley and finished him off in a barrage of bullets and arrows.

After two long days of intense fighting, the eight men left at the mill were smoked out and slaughtered. Among those killed at the battle of Turley's Mill were William Austin, William Hatfield, Joseph Marshall, Peter Robert, Louis Tolque and Albert Turlish. All, including Turley, are buried in a common grave at the Kit Carson Cemetery in Taos.

Today, the rubble of what remains of Turley's Mill sleeps quietly in the depths of the "hidden valley." Chamisa, sagebrush, cactus and timothy blanket the reddish-brown stones that once served as the stout foundations of the thriving mill and distillery. Winding paths about the site are lined with massive boulders; a number are carved with ancient Indian petroglyphs. Quarter horses graze by the Río Hondo, which swirls its way over lichen-covered cobblestones and down into the swirling Río Grande Gorge. The visitor to the site can find no evidence of thirty-gallon barrels of "Taos Lightning," the hoof-prints of mule trains carrying their precious cargo or the trappers trading their beaver pelts. The only thing left is the tranquillity that has settled over the desolate Arroyo Hondo Valley.

Taos Ski Valley
Ernie Blake's Alpine Dream Comes True

Driving north in winter from Taos Plaza, past Indian Pueblo land where buffalo graze, turning right at the "blinking light" and passing through the hamlet of Arroyo Seco, the ski buff enters through a slot that the rushing Río Hondo carved out of a 5,000 foot-deep canyon dense with icicle-covered fir trees. The winding road takes the traveler past Amizett, a boom town in 1893 when the lure of gold held its sway and where Al Helphinstine and his wife, Amizett, fixed up an old cabin for a hotel and established a post office. Climbing up the road to 9,207 feet above sea level, one arrives at a quaint European-style village punctuated by a Swiss-like steepled structure brightly painted by George Chacon with medieval murals. This is Taos Ski Valley, nestled in the Sangre de Cristo Mountains and hidden behind a snow-clad 12,481-foot-high peak called Kachina.

Taos Ski Valley was founded by the energetic and adventurous Ernie Blake, born Ernest Hermann Block in 1913 in Frankfurt, Germany. Blake adopted his code name during World War II when he was attached to General George Patton's Third Army. There his dangerous duties involved clandestine chases, tracking down and interrogating top Third Reich officers hiding in the Bavarian Mountains. Moving from Switzerland to the United States after the war, Blake eventually found his way to New Mexico, where he served first as the general manager of the Santa Fe Ski Basin. Still, his ultimate destiny was to develop a ski mountain he could call his own.

Accompanied by longtime friend Peter Totemoff, an Aleut Indian and ski instructor, Ernie began systematic aerial searches for the perfect location while flying his Cessna 170 between Santa Fe and Glenwood Springs, Colorado, where he managed the two ski areas. After studying stacks of aerial photographs, the two finally decided on a long-abandoned copper mining camp called Twining, which had carved out a rough-and-tumble history of its own.

In 1884, William Frazer, a Colorado miner, opened the Copper Mountain Mine that later came to be the economic hub of the Taos area. A tram road was built so mules could pull the ore from the mine high above the town. Frazer convinced a New Jersey investment banker, Albert Twining, to finance his mining operation. Twining agreed, with his sole reward being that the town and the small hotel in the valley were named after him. Here the miners built dozens of log cabins, thanks to Brigham Young's son, Jesse, who established a sawmill near the mine. When Twining went bankrupt, Frazer took sole possession of the mine. Later in 1910, he, too, on the brink of becoming dead broke, received a loan of $2,000 from Taos banker C.A. Probert and John Bidwell, a Colorado miner. These funds kept him solvent for the time being. Then in 1914, during a violent argument between Bidwell and Frazer, shots were fired. Bidwell was "quicker on the draw" and killed Frazer instantly. Later, acquitted of murder charges on the plea of self-defense, Bidwell left and the mine closed down for good.

Half a century later, in May 1954, Blake and Totemoff scouted the Twining Camp area on foot and on skis and determined that this was the perfect place for an Alpine ski resort. With the help of a crew of eighteen Indians and one mule, they placed a 2000-foot diesel-driven T-Bar in operation one year later. It wasn't too long afterwards that the Taos Ski Valley, a quiet cocoon in northern New Mexico, with steep descents and trails named after Mexican martyrs, Greek gods and German generals killed attempting to assassinate Adolph Hitler, began to attract the ski *cognoscenti* from every corner of the globe.

More of an enclave than a village or town, Taos Ski Valley covers a snug quarter-square-mile at the base of a world-class mountain. It encompasses the base resort center, a cluster of lodges like the Edelweiss, St. Bernard, Thunderbird and The Inn at Snakedance. The latter was originally the

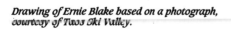

Drawing of Ernie Blake based on a photograph, courtesy of Taos Ski Valley.

Hondo Lodge, built back in the 1940s with timbers from the old miners' cabins. The Ernie Blake Ski School in the valley has been ranked number one in the nation, receiving top honors for its programs teaching all levels of skiers to ski their best. Rhoda's Restaurant, named for Ernie's wife, is famous for its cuisine and its celebrated Martini Tree cocktail bar, a favorite haunt of *aprés* skiers. While not an extensive ski area, Taos Valley is an alpine oasis of never-ending brilliant sunshine and azure skies. It is blanketed with the lightest powder imaginable. It is an exciting, varied terrain with flocks of friendly people. Partially located in Carson National Forest, it offers those who want to venture off the beaten path some of the greatest skiing in North America.

The first trail the new arrival spots heading into the valley is the formidable, mogul-filled, free-fall known as "Al's Run," named for Dr. Al Rosen. He was a Taos local who skied the lift-line run with an oxygen bottle strapped to his back after failing health took his breath away. At the top of the chair lift, skiers are treated to the spectacular view of Wheeler Peak, New Mexico's highest at 13,161 feet. From this vantage point, they can choose from an extensive menu of challenges. The mountain has 72 slopes—36 expert, 19 intermediate and 17 beginner—and 1,092 acres of skiing covered by 312 inches of average annual snowfall, one of the highest in the U.S., and a vertical drop of 2,612 feet. There are gentle slopes, like Honeysuckle and Totemoff that meander down the mountainside, long groomed "cruising" runs, pristine open bowls and gut-wrenching slopes. The more challenging trails include Inferno, Lorelei and the Valkryies Bowl. The one-hour hike to Kachina Peak ranks as one of the ultimate ski experiences. The ridge from the windswept summit down the snowy slot into the powdery chutes of upper Hunzinker Bowl is a favorite Alpine run for seasoned skiers.

Irascible and loquacious, the lovable Ernie Blake was determined to make Taos Ski Valley a success. When his certified public accountant told him to get out of the risky ski business as fast as he could, Ernie immediately changed financial advisors. Today, the valley remains unchanged from the time when Coronado's conquistadores came by in 1540. Framed by giant Engelmann spruce and corkbark fir, heavy with snow on all trail sides, it is a small, intimate, special place for superlative skiing.

During the summer and early fall, before the snow flies, a trek from the valley up the Phoenix Switchback into Wheeler Peak Wilderness is a nature lover's delight. Along the pine-needled, carpeted path, through towering pines and aspens turning 14-karat gold, the hiker encounters scurrying chipmunks and gray jays swooping down from tree branches to peck at trail mix from the palm of the hand. Ernie Blake said, "I pray there is no reincarnation. Nothing could equal the journey I've had. And anything else would be a boring encore." Blake passed away in 1989, and his ashes were scattered from a plane high over his beloved mountain. He had a recipe for the success of his ski valley: "Stir in a full measure of European style, a cupful of Southwestern flavor, bowls of featherlight snow, all served on the slopes of breathtaking mountains." An exception in the corporate world of skiing, the Taos Ski Valley is still family-run. Ernie's son, Mickey Blake, with wife and children are staunchly committed to maintaining the pure Alpine ski experience envisioned by the resort's beloved founder. Every year when the ski season opens in November in the Taos Ski Valley, Ernie's dream comes true once again. The high point of the season is Ernie Blake's Birthday Celebration on March 25 and 26. During these two days of fun are held the Molson Race with obstacles for all levels of skiers, dazzling displays of fireworks, a rock 'n' roll *aprés* ski party, the Ski Challenge Prize Giveaway and an awards ceremony. All this is topped off by a torchlight parade and a mountain treasure hunt with great prizes. It's no wonder Taos Ski Valley ranks in the top 10 of the entire world!

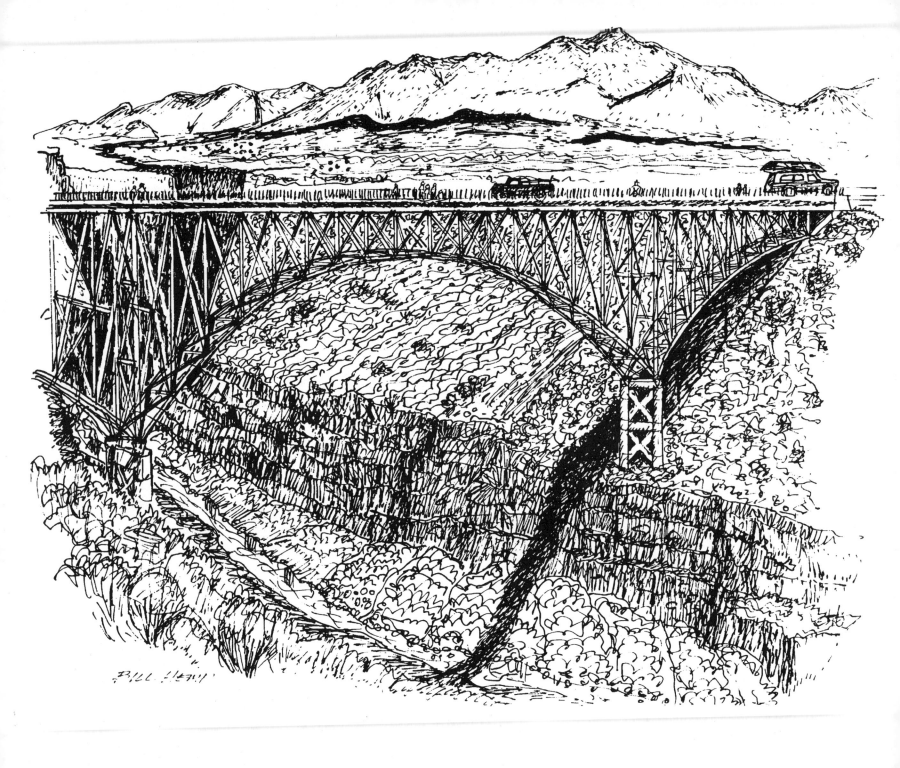

Río Grande Gorge and Bridge

Wild and Scenic Rapids Through Basalt Boulders

Historians tell an old tale of a suave Spanish conquistador commanding his Indian host, who was offering gifts of cotton blankets and food, "Please show me your greatest treasure." The Indian gestured for the Spaniard and his armored retinue to follow. They came to a halt on the grassy banks of a great river. "This is the most precious thing in life," responded the Indian through an interpreter. He pointed toward the glistening waters of what was to be called the Río Grande by the Spanish explorers. The mighty river shimmered a golden hue in the setting sunlight. This ancient legend clearly illustrates how much New Mexicans value their water. In fact, they feel that every drop is a precious gift from the heavens, not to be squandered. Every river, stream, lake and pond is a priceless treasure.

Driving westward across the Taos plateau today on U.S. 64, through a wilderness of silvery-gray sagebrush dotted by clusters of *chamisa*, *piñón* and juniper, the traveler hardly expects to come upon a yawning, wild river gorge slicing its way across the rolling landscape. But that's what happens as one drives across the Río Grande Gorge Bridge. The second highest arch in the United States, it soars two thousand feet from rim to rim, 650 feet above the river.

A formidable obstacle to east-west travel, the deep gorge was avoided by early explorers, military expeditions and immigrants. The trip across the narrow abyss once took hours of slow travel on a winding switchback of a dirt road, down one side and up the other. The John Dunn Bridge, dating from the early 1900s, was the only river-level crossing in the Taos Box section of the Río Grande. Two miles south of the Dunn Bridge, at Manby Springs, are traces of an old wagon road that went into the river. This was known to old-timers as *La Bajada del Caballo*, the "descent of the horse." At the bottom of the great gorge, the Río Grande plows through; its tons of water swirl, splash and boom against slick, black basalt boulders. The desert breeze, moving through the steel beams of the bridge supported on two pylons anchored on the shoulders of the cliffs, blends with the muted sound of the river drifting upward from far below. As it has for centuries, the canyon gorge serves as a magnet for wildlife—golden eagles, great blue heron, snowy egrets, deer and pumas. Coyotes cover a broad territory throughout the gorge. They prefer small game such as rodents and rabbits and carry on in a loud, raucous, yipping chorus. Red-tailed hawks soar above the chasm, catching the warm up-drafts in their search for similar game.

The Río Grande is the nation's second-longest river, after the Missouri-Mississippi. It extends 1,885 miles from its headwaters in the San Juan Mountains of Colorado through the spectacularly deep canyon near Taos, bisects the entire state of New Mexico and passes through Texas to empty its waters in the Gulf of Mexico. Since the days of the Anasazi, the fabled river has served as the lifeblood of New Mexico, irrigating farmlands and providing fertile fields for corn, squash and beans. Its deep pools are the habitat of trophy-sized rainbow and brown trout, cutthroat, catfish and northern pike and a good reason for bait and fly fishermen to undertake the 600-foot hike down into the spectacular canyon.

The La Junta Overlook in the Río Grande Wild Rivers Recreation Area near Questa provides a magnificent view of the confluence of the Red River and the Río Grande. The solitude of the canyon floor, combined with the beauty of the canyon rim above and the white rushing water framed by towering ponderosa below, is a sight long to be remembered by those venturing into the canyon. In early morning, the hiker in the Wild Rivers Parkland might catch sight of the big-eared mule deer or elk, most often spotted along the northern stretches of the River Gorge near Ute Mountain.

Rapids and dashing currents, the unexpected and exciting challenges of the river, attract white-water rafters to parts of the gorge. The Río Grande offers a broad range of floating opportunities, including mild and tranquil segments for the novice and wild, uncontrolled, extremely dangerous stretches that may exceed the skills of the expert. Every year when winter snows melt and the water is high, the Río Grande Gorge is suddenly populated by thousands of white-water enthusiasts who raft, kayak and canoe with wild abandon.

From the Colorado border to the Taos Junction Bridge, the gorge is often called America's first "Wild and Scenic River," to be preserved untouched. The "Upper Taos Box," rated a Class V-Plus, is reserved specifically for expert kayakers who fully understand the risks involved. One of the most exhilarating white-water river rides is the "Lower Taos Box," a sixteen-mile section of the gorge classified by an act of Congress as "Wild and Scenic." Rafters in paddle boats plunge down a chasm that drops as much as ninety feet per mile through the *Río Bravo* and through a continuous four-mile stretch of Class III (moderately difficult) to Class IV (boiling and bubbling) high-water rapids. Rafters finish the stretch with their jaws hanging open and their bodies thoroughly drenched.

At the steel-beamed John Dunn Bridge located in the rocky labyrinth of Arroyo Hondo Canyon

north of Taos, rafters who "put in" for the Lower Taos Box experience some of the loveliest and wildest water anywhere in New Mexico. Rated a Class IV run, which means exceptionally difficult for experts, the stretch through the gorge and its "Powerline Falls" is described as one of the most spectacular rapids on the Río Grande or any other river. Below the Box, the river flows through the Orilla Verde Recreation Area, near the snug village of Pilar, a quiet float of six miles distance. It then winds through an area called the "Race Course," consisting of five miles of Class III rapids like Albert Falls, The Narrows, Dead Foot, Big Rock and Godzilla. This race course provides thrills for families throughout the season, going past 1500-foot high cliffs of quartzite on the east and basalt on the west and ending at the Taos-Río Arriba County Line.

At historic Embudo Station, which once served as the terminus for the "Chile Line" narrow-gauge railway from Colorado, bone-tired, water-soaked rafters can satisfy their "wet and wild" appetites over dinner at the tree-shaded cafe overlooking the shimmering river. Embudo Station was where John Wesley Powell established the nation's first water-measuring station.

Today visitors departing the Taos Valley region and heading west toward Arizona on U.S. 64 can cross the Río Grande Gorge Bridge in a matter of seconds. Or they can park and walk across, pausing at mid-span to stare dizzyingly down, testing their equilibrium. The river swirls through basalt boulders far below. This convenient passage of time is a far cry from the early days of this century, when travelers on "Long" John Dunn's rusty stagecoaches had to make the trip by way of scary switchbacks down into the precipitous canyon and across a rickety old bridge over the Río Grande. Those were the days!

BILL HEMP

The Enchanted Circle
Ghost Towns of the Glittering Gold Rush

For a trip back in time to the "boom or bust" days of the raw frontier, complete with mountain vistas, deep canyons, surging streams and the verdant Carson National Forest, nothing can surpass the 85-mile scenic loop called "The Enchanted Circle." The panoramic route begins on U.S. 64 and continues east from Taos, taking one through Taos Canyon and up over the 9,000-foot-high Palo Flechado, the pass of the arrow, and down into the sprawling Moreno Valley and Angel Fire.

Now a ski resort, Angel Fire was once the fall meeting grounds of the Moache Ute Indians, a nomadic tribe that gathered at the head of Agua Fría Peak. Legend has it that lightning struck a timber causing a roaring fire that spread quickly across the forested mountains. The Utes called upon their God to save their camp. Soon the sky darkened, the wind reversed direction, it began raining and the fire was extinguished. The winds that had saved the Valley of the Fires became known as the "Breath of Angels," and finally "Angel Fire." According to another story, the area got its name from the glow that permeates the mountains in the late autumn. Kit Carson once mentioned that he supposed it was the sun reflecting on hoar frost through the evergreen branches on the far horizon.

Nearby, on the crest of a hill, rises the stark, wing-shaped DAV Vietnam Veterans National Memorial erected by Dr. Victor Westphall in 1968, in memory of his son, David, who lost his life at an ambush site on May 22, 1968. The intimate chapel appears to have arms that offer a gesture of welcome for living Vietnam veterans and those who could not come home.

Going northeast off U.S. 64, the traveler arrives at Eagle Nest, a tiny hamlet scattered alongside a 78,000-acre lake, created in 1916 by Charles Springer, who built a huge concrete dam at the head of Cimarron Canyon. Today, Eagle Nest Lake lures trout fishermen and windsurfers in summer and ice fishermen and snowmobilers in winter. During warm-weather months the winds can whip up on a moment's notice, creating giant waves. To protect boats and fishermen from being swamped by the 15-foot-high waves, a siren alarm system has been set up to give them time to reach the safety of the shore.

About four miles north of Eagle Nest on Route 38, a left turn onto a dirt road takes one to the site of Elizabethtown, a frontier mining camp that sprang up during the frantic rush when gold was discovered in Willow Creek. In 1866, fortune seekers were taken in by the cry of "Thar's gold in them thar hills!" They came hoping to strike it rich. In 1866, a wounded Indian rescued by a Union Army soldier, John Moore, and recovering at Fort Union, "The Guardian of the Santa Fe Trail," offered his gratitude by giving Moore some "pretty rocks." Recognizing them as copper-bearing, Moore set out for Baldy Mountain, where rich deposits were soon discovered, resulting in the mine known as "The Mystic Lode."

Yet it was the deposits of gold first panned in Willow Creek and then in almost every creekbed and *arroyo* in the area that brought the throngs of thirsty Gold Rushers to the valley.

In 1868, Moore and other miners platted out a townsite. Moore named it Elizabethtown, after his daughter. Water for solid mining was brought from Red River via the "Big Ditch" project, said to be one of the most remarkable engineering feats of its day. The site was destined to become the richest gold-producing area in New Mexico. The "Aztec Lode" netted over five million dollars in the mineral, with outlying mining camps like Baldy, near the top of a barren mountain in the Alpine wilderness, and Virginia City hauling in their share of the profits.

Elizabethtown is nestled in the Moreno Valley with 12,441-foot-high Baldy Mountain on the east and Wheeler Peak, named for a U.S. surveyor and attaining 13,161 feet—the highest in New Mexico—on the west. E-town, as it was nicknamed by the miners, listed a population of about 5,000 people, enough to support five stores, seven saloons, a drug store, three dance halls and two hotels, one of which was owned by Herman Mutz, a rancher. The rose-colored granite ruins of the Mutz Hotel still stand today. Its picturesque, arched windows look out longingly over the weeded, abandoned town. Not far below stand the ramshackle remains of Herman Froelich's General Store and Butcher Shop, festooned with skulls and antlers of deer and elk. Jack Biemer, who grew up in E-town, remembers his father, who was the sheriff, saying when buying wild game there, "Herman, take your damn finger off that scale!"

In September of 1903, a disastrous fire broke out in E-town, quickly engulfing the saloons, stores and miners' cabins. It was a hard blow for the mining camp, a blow from which it never recovered. Today Elizabethtown remains a ghost town, hugging the windswept hillside, where quarter horses, shaggy mules and cattle of different colors graze in the prairie land beside a stream. The rock foundations of once-bustling buildings are still visible through clumps of gray *chamisa*. Only the wind whistling through the rotting logs of cabins and the swooping of magpies disturb the quiet. The ghost town enjoys a deep sleep after all those riotous years during the rip-roaring days of the Gold Rush. Visitors who stroll around the area through the granite rubble of the hotel and by the dilapidated general store can revive in their wild imagination the lusty miners, the smoke-filled saloon halls and the talks of gold strikes, thus reliving a bit of the past in the old frontier mining camp in the hills near Baldy Peak.

Proceeding northwest on U.S. 38, the loop heads over Bobcat Pass down into Red River, a miners' boomtown in the 1890s. The settlement got its name from the mountain stream whose mineral content gave it a rich shade of rosy red. Platted in 1895, Red River soared to 3,000 people with "get rich quick" fever, and the good and the bad moved in by the dozens to support an active red-light district. Copper, gold and silver mines were kept busy in the area in the years leading up to 1925. The major mines were located in Bitter Creek, Goose Creek, Pioneer, Mallette and Upper Red River Canyon.

The town's first log-cabin schoolhouse, with Mrs. Ida Phipps as the teacher, opened in 1890 but burned down in 1915. It was replaced by the Red School House in the same year. It still stands, boasting a fresh coat of fire-engine red paint. Today, Red River, the highest town in the state of New Mexico, at an altitude of 8,750 feet, offers sports enthusiasts thirty-three ski trails and five chair lifts. Just a few miles east, in the Enchanted Forest Cross-Country Ski and Snow Shoe Touring Center, Nordic trekkers and wildlife watchers can enjoy well-groomed trails under towering pines heavy with pristine snow.

Heading west on NM 38, the Enchanted Circle then meanders through scenic Red River Canyon, dotted with aspen, Englemann spruce and ponderosa pine, before arriving at Questa a quiet village settled in 1840. (*Cuesta*, which means hill, was once misspelled by a postman and now the town bears the name Questa.) Here, amid

some of the most spectacular scenery in the state, with spell-binding Flag Mountain to the east, one can visit the Red River State Trout Hatchery. Colorful rainbow trout are raised here for stocking New Mexico's lakes, ponds and streams.

The circle continues back toward the Taos plateau, heading south on Route 522, past Lama and the locale in San Cristóbal of the D. H. Lawrence Ranch. Heading down into Taos, "the Soul of the Southwest," past the Taos Indian Reservation and the sacred Pueblo Peak, the "circle" is complete. It is a fabulous journey that has taken the traveler deep into the "Land of Enchantment."

D.H. Lawrence Ranch

Lorenzo, Frieda and Friend on Mount Lobo

On Route 522 about twenty miles above Taos, a small sign on the right-hand side of the road directs the traveler to the D.H. Lawrence Ranch, which lies above the San Cristóbal Valley. The five-mile-long stretch of dirt road up the side of Lobo Mountain leads to the rustic and remote "Flying Heart Ranch." Mabel Dodge Luhan, who had lured Lawrence to Taos, gave the ranch to his German wife, Frieda, a distant cousin of the "Red Baron" Von Richtofhen, World War I flying ace. She, in return, presented Mabel with the original handwritten manuscript of Lawrence's celebrated novel, *Sons and Lovers*. Several years later the great bundle of finely written pages that Lawrence had sweated over long ago was presented by Mabel to A.A. Brill, a psychoanalyst, as payment for helping a close friend.

Here, on the 160-acre property, which Lawrence immediately renamed "Lobo," wolf, after the mountain behind it, then changed later to "Kiowa," after the Indian trail used by the Taos Pueblo Indians traveling on horseback, the author and his wife, with whom he had eloped in 1913, spent many pleasant but volatile days between 1924 and 1925. Lawrence described Taos as "a tiny place 30 miles from the railway, high up—7,000 feet in the desert—so one's heart pit-a-pats a bit."

Lawrence and Frieda found two semiderelict log cabins with no plumbing next to each other inside a picket fence. They cleaned and painted the cabins. In the smaller cabin, just big enough for a cot, table, chair and trunk, resided the Honorable Dorothy Brett, British daughter of the 2nd Viscount of Esher. Brett, as she was called, had studied portrait painting in London and had followed D. H. to New Mexico. She worked like a monk at the writer's right arm, typing, while Frieda lay on the bed, chain-smoking her eternal, extra-long cigarettes. Slightly deaf, Brett always carried a brass ear trumpet, which she called "Toby," in order to hear what her talented circle of friends were talking about. During her stay with the Lawrences, Brett adopted a costume for the Southwest consisting of a wide-brimmed *sombrero*, high boots and a pair of men's corduroy trousers. Stashed in the side of her right boot was a sharp *stiletto* for protection. As a result, the local Spanish-speaking people were afraid of her, with one hired hand on the ranch saying, "*Señorita* with dagger very dangerous."

During the time Lawrence spent at the ranch, less than two years, he was 8,500 feet up in comparative isolation on the forested mesa with its towering protective pines and sloping fields filled with lavender columbines and cobalt-blue lupines. The author went about doing the things he most enjoyed. He wrote in the morning after he had finished such chores as chopping wood, milking Susan, the cow, and baking bread in the *horno* he had built himself. Later, after riding his horse, Azul, and playing with his pet cat, Timsy Wemsyss, he would sit in the shade of a pine tree and, with his student exercise notebook on his knees, using a big-barreled, red fountain pen to rapidly fill the pages in a beautifully legible script with hardly a change. After he wrote, the faithful, adoring Brett would type up the day's work or go out with her brushes, easel and palette to paint canvases of the lovely Lobo landscape.

From time to time, Lawrence was prevailed upon to attend one of the elaborate parties at "Mabeltown," the name he bestowed on the Luhan hacienda, where his stormy disposition usually affected everyone who came in close contact with him. But when he remained aloof from the possessive clutches of Mabel, whom he described as a "culture carrier with a terrible will-to-power," Lawrence was able to complete his book, *The Plumed Serpent*, and the novella, *St. Mawr*, which accurately described the Kiowa Ranch and its rich history. It was his habit to use his wife, friends and acquaintances as models for his fictional characters: Frieda in *The Plumed Serpent*, Brett in *The Princess*, and Mabel in *The Woman Who Rode Away*. A number of *Taoseños* appear in the works written during his brief stay in New Mexico.

(Drawing of D.H. Lawrence adapted from a photograph courtesy of La Fonda de Taos Hotel.)

Lawrence's marriage to Frieda and their subsequent move to New Mexico separated her from her English exhusband, Weekley, and their children. The marital relationship of Lawrence and Frieda was not without its ups and downs. At tea one time in a friend's house, D.H. suddenly attacked his wife: "Frieda, don't be stupid. I should slap you for that!" She instantly struck back: "I can't be so dumb when you quote me all the time in your books." One morning, with the physically ill author spitting blood, a frightened Frieda called Doc Martin, Taos' only physician, who after a two-hour journey to the ranch from town, arrived in his "Tin Lizzie" with black satchel and dusty thermometer in hand, to tend the writer. His advice was to "keep him in bed!"

Extremely jealous of Brett and her over-zealous attention to Lawrence, Frieda, for weeks at a time, forbade Dorothy to visit the ranch. But Brett survived and went on to live out a full life in New Mexico, painting Indians, their dances and ceremonies. She had been fascinated by Native Americans ever since the time when, at the age of five, she attended Buffalo Bill's Wild West Show in London and fell in love with a wild young Indian brave riding bareback, whooping and gesturing with a feather-festooned spear. A Taos resident for the rest of her days, she lived to the ripe old age of ninety-four, passing away in 1977 and leaving her hearing aid behind to pique the interest of visitors to the ranch.

Today, a hike up a flagstone path toward Lobo Peak through parallel groves of blue-gray spruce and ponderosa pines, leads to the D. H. Lawrence Shrine, a grotto-like dwelling designed by Angelino Ravagli, Frieda's third husband. Here, the ashes of the tortured, shrill-voiced author, who passed away in 1930 of tuberculosis in a sanitarium at Vence, an ancient Roman stronghold in the foothills of the Maritime Alps in the south of France, are interred. Documents certifying his death and the shipment of his remains across the Atlantic on the Italian liner, *Conte de Savoia*, hang on the shrine's wall. As was her last wish, Frieda is buried just outside, her grave marked by a large snow-white slab etched with her name in large block letters.

Without Frieda's exuberance and vitality, Lawrence would most probably have succumbed years earlier, without having penned his Southwest classics, crowned by *The Plumed Serpent*. But Frieda refused to take any credit in her event-filled memoirs, which she called *Not I, But The Wind*.

It has been seven decades since the blue-eyed, red-bearded genius, whom Mabel Dodge Luhan likened to "St. John, The Baptist" penned his manuscripts high up on the pine-shaded mountains above the Taos Valley. Yet hundreds of Lawrence readers and *aficionados* drive the rutted road up to the ranch seeking to pay their respects at the shrine built in his memory. A small registry book is inscribed with name after name, including scribbled personal remarks praising his novels, poetry and plays. While the controversial author of *Lady Chatterly's Lover* had been happier at the ranch above Taos than in any other place, so said his wife in her throaty, smoky tones, the pull to go elsewhere was too strong to resist. So, he set out for the south of France where he spent the final days of his forty, talented, tormented but fruitful years on this planet earth. *Ciao*, Lorenzo!

BILL HEMP

New Buffalo "Back To The Land" Commune
Hippie Culture Congregates at Arroyo Hondo

Motoring seven miles north from Taos to Arroyo Hondo and hanging a left at Herb's Lounge, then heading westward on Lower Hondo Road toward the Río Grande Gorge, the traveler enters into an ancient valley of small farms and a buffalo ranch sliced by a sparkling stream. Climbing up a bumpy road, one discovers, at the crest of a hill, a scattering of tepees with thin folds of smoke rising out of their air vents, surrounding a zia-shaped complex of adobe buildings. This is New Buffalo, New Mexico's first "hippie" commune, which galvanized public attention in the 1960s, well before Woodstock. It was in the beehive-roofed central chamber that communards took their meals, held meetings and partied, earning New Buffalo the reputation as the "hippiest" crash pad in the colorful Southwest.

This is the legendary shrine of "Let's Learn How to Live Together" that provided inspiration for the movie, *Easy Rider*. This is where Captain America and Billy took a break from their long trip to eat rice and score some acid. This is where Captain America smoked a joint, leaned against an adobe wall and said, "I'm hip about time." This is where white-robed Timothy Leary—"Turn on, Tune in, Drop out!"—came to call, arriving in Taos in a three-engine French airplane. This is where Aquarius Paul mixed mud and straw to make adobe bricks and where people who felt alienated trekked from all over to be part of the movement that would change the world. Some had migrated to New Mexico from the gloss and the froth, the concrete anonymity of New York. Some were California "hippies" who fled inland to escape the inevitable earthquake along the St. Andreas Fault that would send San Francisco and points north and south sliding into the Pacific. Some were ex-motorcyclists or artists or former *habitués* of Haight-Ashbury who ardently believed in the anticapitalist credo. Their appearance was fairly standard—long-haired. The men sported scruffy Rutherford B. Hayes beards; their "chicks" were beaded and outfitted mildly outlandishly. Gazing across the Hondo Valley's majestic landscape, one barefooted beatnik observed, "New Mexico may be the last real expression of the alternative way of life." At a time when seventy percent of America's people were living jammed together on one percent of its surface, suddenly a new generation of young people began to flow out in the opposite direction—out where fish leap and forest rangers roam and "Smokey The Bear" is king of the mountain. The city-bred migrants discovered that New Mexico's open country can produce a natural "high" as psychedelic as any chemical. They found a sense of "self" emerging from the mythical essence of the land and from each soul's new unfettered impulses. The land and its expanded immensity of unbroken horizon became a key to the communards' search for another style of being.

New Buffalo was officially launched under the leadership of Max Feinstein and Rick Klein as an International Community (commune) on the first day of summer 1967, by hippies who either bypassed or had outgrown Haight-Ashbury. Here in northern New Mexico they realized they could grow and farm and simultaneously probe the potentials of a fresh relationship between man and earth—all in exquisite rural seclusion. The commune, with an awesome view of the Sangre de Cristo Mountains to the east, was financed from an inheritance received by 25-year-old Rick Klein, a talented musician who wanted to get as far away as possible from his button-down Pittsburgh, Pennsylvania, upbringing. The commune's first president was Princeton graduate Robert Calvin Gordon, III. The place was named after the Indians' provider—the buffalo. It had no structure—only a strong "work your ass off" ethic and a spiritual base built on Peyote ceremonies learned from local members of the Native American Church, especially Grandpa Joe Gomez of Taos Pueblo. The "Buffalos" farmed on about 30 of their 103 acres, cultivating soybeans, corn, wheat, barley and millet plus small patches of pumpkins, onions, lettuce, tomatoes and other vegetables for everyday consumption.

Rick Klein left after the first year and moved up the road to Lama. The original founders stayed on, hauling drinking water from the nearby *acequia*, building adobe dwellings, adding chambers and turning everything into a work of art, be it a bus, a car or the side of a barn. Physical labor was expected. "Learn or die" was the byword. Land was tilled and gardened without chemicals. Fresh vegetables and whole grains became daily food staples. Pottery, batik, beadwork, tie-dye, silver, leather and jewelry-making moved from individual interests into full-scale craft industries. Wearing bizarre clothing, just letting it all hang out or bathing bare-ass naked in the nearby Río Grande Hot Springs was an expression of one's own creativity.

To the Spanish-Americans living in the Taos Valley since Oñate's settler days of the 17th century, this whole hippie colonization movement represented an influx of especially offensive Anglo "freak people," whose appearance and lifestyle seemed a deliberate mockery of everything they had been striving for in life. The relationship between *Taoseños* and the "unwanted" newcomers was not a pleasant one, with a number of confrontations resulting in violence and threats to burn the place to the ground. But as 1968 turned into 1973, the hippies either drifted away or were slowly absorbed into the multicultural magic of Taos itself, and the battle between the two opposite forces subsided. One of the few communes to survive to this day is the Lama Foundation, near Questa, with a scattering of geodesic domes inspired by Buckminster Fuller. By 1980, the wonder of New Buffalo began to fade. Land and buildings designed to sustain a handful of hard-working families were overrun by drifters and dreamers, up to 40 a day, who shoplifted and ruined the reputation of the dedicated communards. Over time, people left to make their own lives. In the mid-1980s, one family had stayed on, struggling to raise goats and crops. Then, some years later, when the occupants moved away, the property was rented for an agricultural research experiment followed by an alternative high school.

In early 1992, Rick Klein and his wife, Terry, returned to New Buffalo and, after much thought, decided then to convert the crumbling Hondo commune into a bed-and-breakfast inn. "This place is historic," Klein observed. "This is where the hippies met the Indians."

Today guests enter the hilltop inn through a greenhouse flanking the main adobe building. The greenhouse provides shafts of warm sunlight in winter for the profusion of flowers growing in tubs inside. But the big treat in store for new arrivals is the Buffalo Room, the cavernous common room featuring a lofty ceiling supported by massive mahogany-brown *vigas* and a hogan-style roof with eleven skylights. The space is sunk into the earth in the fashion of a Taos Pueblo *kiva*. This exotic venue is dominated by a giant stuffed head of the shaggy provider buffalo, who casts his beady brown eyes around the room from over the door. It is used for playing music, beating Indian drums, displaying local artists'

sculptures and paintings, meditations, dining and gathering. Besides offering modern amenities, guest rooms are tastefully decorated with original art from commune days: mosaics, mandalas and South American weavings, which Terry Klein restored and preserved. The medieval-like "Tower Room" offers modern-day Romeos and Juliets a luxuriant sleeping loft, a view of the valley and pristine walls painted with white clay that contains minute flakes of glistening mica, creating a romantic mood. Strolling about the commune-turned-inn one finds on the *vigas* and in the nooks and crannies engraved spirited messages of earlier times, such as "Live in Joy and Peace," framed psychedelic posters, tie-dye wall hangings, tiles and sculptures "mudded" into the walls.

Opened on Christmas Eve 1992, the New Buffalo now serves as a bed and breakfast inn and a retreat center. "No Alcohol or Drugs Allowed" says the sign as the guest gears up the washboard road to the tepee-dotted commune grounds. Nowadays the inn attracts visitors from cities and towns across the country and around the world. Not surprisingly, many of the most appreciative visitors turn out to be teens and young adults. Terry explained, "They feel that they missed being a part of the 1960s and they're really curious." Rick Klein added, "This place partakes of that Taos mystique. It always did." And it still does!

The Frank Waters Foundation
Aspen-Son Under The Mountain

In 1947 a lean, handsome man walked up a dusty road from the tiny village of Arroyo Seco. He was intent on exploring an ancient cave and waterfall reputed once to have been used by Indians of Taos Pueblo in their ceremonies. On the way he stopped a moment to admire a small, abandoned adobe surrounded by cottonwoods growing along a narrow stream flowing between the house and the road. Later, through discreet inquiries, he found that the house was owned by Josephine Cordova, who was having problems keeping up the property. The lone wanderer eventually met Josephine and purchased the two-room dwelling along with 15 adjacent acres. Thus began the Taos adventure of Frank Waters, the legendary writer, and his inspiring 150-year-old adobe house. The Indians used to call the area *La Isla*, because it was surrounded by water on all four sides.

Frank Waters was born on July 25, 1902, in Colorado Springs, Colorado, the son of Frank Jonathan Waters and May Dozier Waters. At the age of 14, Waters saw his writing published in his grade-school literary magazine. After studying engineering at Colorado College, he worked in the Salt Creek oil fields of Wyoming and later in southern California. Then he saw his first book, *Fever Pitch*, published in 1930. While scratching out a living in Taos in 1939, he penned *People of the Valley*. This earthy novel, describing the lives of the Spanish speaking people of the wide Mora Valley, focused on the primitive but ruthless Maria del Valle. It was pub-lished in 1941. Adding to his growing reputation as a storyteller was the publication in 1942 of *The Man Who Killed The Deer*. This wonderfully perceptive, timeless story tells of pueblo sin and redemption and of the conflict between Indian and white laws. It demonstrates why Waters stands as the foremost storyteller in both fiction and nonfiction of the vast Southwest. Critics have noted that Waters writes out of a long association with the American Indian and the Spanish-American and with a deep understanding of their values and cultures.

From 1959 to 1963 Waters worked on the novel, *Book of the Hopi*, living frugally much of the time on the Hopi reservation. His later works included a biography of the Russian painter, Leon Gaspard, *Woman at Otowi Crossing*, *Pumpkin Seed Point*, and *Pike's Peak*. The latter work was a semiautobiographical novel of three generations of a Colorado family. His carefully researched book, *To Possess The Land*, covered the life and times of the controversial land grant owner and English remittance man Arthur Rochford Manby. Manby was believed to have been murdered and his body was beheaded. The corpse was found by a deputy U.S. marshal who had come to collect from Manby a $14,000 breach-of-promise suit he had lost. In the 1970s and 1980s, Waters pursued his talents by writing and having published *Mountain Dialogues*, *Flight From Fiesta*, and *Eternal Desert*. During this time he was nominated several times for a Nobel Prize for Literature.

Today the visitor who accepts an invitation to the Waters compound in Arroyo Seco comes to a rise in the road heading toward El Salto Mountain, then crosses over a small wooden bridge spanning a stream. Awaiting the guest sprawls an L-shaped adobe dwelling sheltered under a grove of seven slim, white-barked aspens. Behind the house clusters a barn, a colt corral and a shed that protects Frank's trusty red and white 1966 Ford Galaxie that proudly shows 200,000 miles on the odometer. On arriving at the author's residence, one observes hanging on the door a piece of aspen wood on which the noted Japanese painter Michio Takayama, who lived many years in Taos, designated the place as "Home of Aspen-san near the Mountain." Inspired by this simple but lovely gesture, Barbara Hayes Waters, whom the writer married in 1979, always thinks of her husband as "Aspen-son," twin to the seven aspens stretching skyward toward their doubles in Frank's favorite constellation, the Pleiades. They mirror his lucky number, seven.

Inside the comfortable house, a number of precious treasures delight the eye. These include Nicolai Fechin's charcoal study of Frank; an Indian dance painting by Lady Dorothy Brett; an antique *trastero* given to him by Mabel Dodge Luhan in the late 1930s when he left the studio she had temporarily provided him and a massive bed from her villa in Florence, Italy. A quick stop in Frank Waters' studio gives one the rare opportunity to glance at the simple desk where dozens of his spellbinding stories were conceived. On top rests a small, well-used Olivetti typewriter purchased in 1956, a few old books, some sharpened pencils and pens.

Horses have always played a leading role in the Waters' pasture behind the house and barn. In 1993, Frank and Barbara acquired two very handsome Missouri Foxtrotters: Golden Girl and Ginger. "There must be enough Indian in me [he was part Cheyenne] to feel that every man's land should have a horse on it," Frank has written. "An Indian has got to have horses, the more the better, to show his social standing; or perhaps merely because he loves their movement in the static landscape."

Frank's favorite was a small white mare called Cry-Baby. Her mother was a famous bucking mare used in rodeos, and whenever she was let out of the chutes, her colt used to cry for her, hence the name.

"She must have had a strain of Arabian to give her such a beautiful conformation and indomitable spirit," he recalled with a touch of nostalgia. "Cry-Baby was 29 years old when she died."

June of 1994 marked the dedication of the Frank Waters Room in Zimmerman Library's Southwest Center for Research at the University of New Mexico. Featured in the FW Room are Frank's compelling portrait painted by the late Rod Goebel, a bronze bust sculpted by Mark Rossi and the mandolin Frank played in his teens when this instrument was the rage. Two of Nicolai Fechin's original charcoal illustrations from *The Colorado* also have found a home here, along with one of Dorothy Brett's fanciful renditions of the final climb up Taos Sacred Mountain to Blue Lake.

With encroaching development surrounding them in Arroyo Seco, Frank and Barbara Waters took two steps to preserve their land and house from sale and exploitation when they are gone. Barbara, who earned two master's degrees from the University of Arizona, first arranged an easement with the Taos Land Trust, then legally established the precious land as part of the Frank Waters Foundation. This nonprofit organization made its official debut in Santa Fe on June 26, 1993, at an afternoon book-signing by Frank of his newest work, *Brave Are My People*.

Creativity is the keystone of the foundation. Its purpose is to promote the arts by providing persons with inspirational living space in which to work for limited periods. In a sense it is a continuation of Frank Waters' life work, so closely tied to the land. In the years to come, retreat studios will be built on the front and back portions of the Waters' 15 wooded acres. The pristine beauty of the remaining eight acres is protected in perpetuity by the Taos Land Trust. Looming above are the Sangre de Cristo Mountains, including Taos Sacred Mountain, source of inspiration and faith to many. The Frank Waters Foundation is rooted in this faith. The revered author passed away June 3, 1995.

B. H.

(Drawing of Frank Waters after a charcoal study by Nicolai Fechin courtesy of the Frank Waters Foundation.)

Casas, Camposantos and Curiosities

A Leisurely Stroll Back Into Taos Time

Andrew Dasburg Studio

In 1918, Mabel Dodge sent a telegram to Andrew Dasburg (1887-1979) in New York. "Wonderful place. You must come. Am sending tickets. Bring me a cook." When the artist arrived in Taos at sunset on a snowy day, Taos Valley seemed like the first days of creation. While it seemed lonely and far from Paris where he was born and New York where he was a participant in the famous Armory Show of 1913, he felt an instant sense of being a part of the place.

Andrew Dasburg has been described as the greatest draftsman of landscape since Van Gogh. He was a pioneer modernist. His paintings and charcoal drawings of the Taos Valley rank among the finest ever created here. Discovering Cezanne's paintings, watching Matisse at work and meeting Picasso, Andrew went on to create a series of stark but powerful landscapes which earned him new fame as a major artist of the American scene.

Crippled from youth as a result of a near-fatal bout with Addison's disease, he emerged from depression and sickness to move permanently to Ranchos just south of Taos to create such awesome works as *Road into Ranchos de Taos*, *Llano Quemado* and *Trampas Church*.

Every morning at nine o'clock, the aging artist walked out the door of his adobe *casa*, got behind the steering wheel of his pale-green Dodge Dart and drove just 50 yards across the field to his studio to begin work at his easel. At one time he was the lover of the radical, Louise Bryant, portrayed by Diane Keaton in the film, *Reds*. Until his death in 1979, Dasburg made Ranchos de Taos his home. The building is now a bed-and-breakfast. His signature can be seen today scribbled indelibly in stone on the wall of his 19th century studio. It is a simple reminder to visitors of a dynamic and determined artist.

A leading social, literary and artistic figure in early 20th century Taos, Blanche Chloe Grant (1874-1948), a brunette, brown-eyed beauty, is best known for her book, *When Old Trails Were New, The Story of Taos*. Blanche dedicated her popular historical treatise to the memory of two citizens of Taos, "Kit Carson, the Greatest American Scout, and Teresina Bent Scheurich, daughter of Governor Bent, to whom every historian of Taos must be forever indebted." She also included Lewis H. Garrard, "the boy traveler of the Forties who wrote the best book about the Old Taos Trail." The most prolific in writing about the town of Taos, Grant penned the only full-scale history of the vast valley as well as three little paper-covered studies, which she published privately: *One Hundred Years Ago in Old Taos, Taos Today* and *Taos Indians*. As if this were not enough, she guided the first publication on a grand scale of Kit Car-

son's biography. In 1926 Blanche Grant obtained a rare typed copy of Dewitt C. Peter's biography, *Kit Carson's Life and Adventures from Facts Narrated by Himself*, and had the complete work published in Taos in 1926.

Besides being a historian, Grant oftentimes picked up palette and brushes, stepped into her studio and worked at her easel. One of her more important paintings, *The Saddle Blanket*, hangs today at the Harwood Gallery on nearby Ledoux Street. Her portrait of the aging scout, soldier and Indian agent hangs above the fireplace in the living room of the Kit Carson House. After her death in 1948, the abstract painters, Louis Leon Riyak and his wife, Bea Mandelman, took up residence in the cozy adobe above Ranchitos Road that clings tenaciously to a bluff behind the terraced compound of the enchanting Taos Hacienda Inn.

Painted a vivid red-raspberry color with Taos-blue portals, this extraordinary adobe dwelling, situated in Cañon, one mile east of the plaza on Kit Carson Road, was once the palatial home of the renowned Russian painter, Leon Gaspard (1881-1964). Today, the house looms out of a stand of towering cottonwoods and blue spruces looking somewhat like a *dacha* on the outskirts of Moscow. Before he moved to Taos from his native country, Gaspard's life was filled with adventures from his student days in Paris at the Académie Julian and his treks across Mongolia and China. Seriously injured in a fighter plane crash during World War I, Leon came to the Taos Valley to recuperate and never left.

In his north-lighted studio with a view of Pueblo Peak, Gaspard painted from memory the pastel shades, powerful shadows, misty mountains and hazy landscapes so characteristic of northern New Mexico. The Tiwa-speaking Indians at the Taos Pueblo reminded the mustachioed artist of Mongolians,

BILL HEMP

the Indian ponies brought back poignant memories of Chinese horse breeds and the snow-mantled mountain spruces conjured up images of Siberian winters. By the time he came to New Mexico his style was fully formed, akin to impressionism but without the scientific bent of the French, using light and color with great vitality.

His painted *trastero* furniture and other works, such as the oil paintings *The Mongolian Monastery* and *Taos Indians,* reside in the Harwood Gallery. Many of his masterpieces can be seen in private homes scattered throughout the valley. An outsider, Leon Gaspard, who befriended the Connecticut artist Eric Sloane, noted for his meticulous pen-and-ink drawings of barns and covered bridges, was not embraced by the Taos artist colony. But this didn't bother Leon in the least. While he admired their works, he considered his Russian-inspired paintings to be "much more mature."

Born in London, the daughter of Nate Salsbury, the originator and producer of Buffalo Bill's Wild West Show, which starred sharpshooter Annie Oakley, Rebecca, or "Beck" as she was called by friends, first summered in Taos in 1929 with Georgia O'Keeffe. The two women had strong-boned faces and made a striking pair—Georgia mannishly dressed all in black and Beck with intense sapphire-blue eyes and prematurely white hair. When Georgia sold a painting for $6,000, she immediately bought a shiny black Model A Ford in Taos. Beck then got the dubious honor of teaching Georgia to drive. She clutched frantically at the front passenger seat as the aloof artist propelled her machine faster and faster along *arroyos* and over rickety bridges. Rebecca's paintings on glass of Victorian-style bouquets were shown in New York at the American Place Gallery owned by O'Keeffe's husband, Alfred Stieglitz. A familiar sight around Taos with her silver-haired page boy, black western hat and black cape, she wrote a popular little book in 1953 called *Allow Me to Present 18 Ladies & Gentlemen of Taos, N.M., 1885-1939*. It was crammed with biographical sketches of the leading personalities of town including doughBelly Price and Ralph Meyers. Following her first marriage to Paul Strand, the movie maker and noted photographer, she then wed Bill James, who came from a prominent New Mexico ranching, banking and mining family.

In her later years Beck was celebrated for her *colcha* embroidery work, used throughout northern New Mexico during the Spanish-Colonial era, which she revived and vigorously promoted. She named her charming adobe on Bent Street "*Casa Felíz*" (Happy House), and the words may still be seen today carved in the lintel above the front window. On the front door of *Casa Felíz* one can admire a painting of Our Lady of Guadalupe, which is believed to have come from an old Taos Valley church torn down years ago. Just up the street is the territorial-style home of Ferdinand Maxwell, a prosperous merchant and Indian agent to the Apache tribe during the Civil War.

Quietly exploring this well-maintained graveyard off Pueblo Road, one gets the opportunity to examine the engravings on the marble and granite gravestones of many notables who wrote the 19th- and 20th-century history of Taos. After the 1847 Rebellion, Doña Teodora Martínez Romero donated land at the northern edge of town to bury the honored dead. Dubbed *El Cemeterio Militia*, its name was changed to the "American Cemetery" in 1852. Then, in 1868, Christopher "Kit" Carson, scout and soldier, died in Fort Lyons, Colorado. He was buried there, then interred in Boggsville. Later, his body was brought home to Taos and buried next to that of his wife. As a result, in 1869, the graveyard was named the "Kit Carson Cemetery."

Prominent citizens interred in the grounds read like a veritable "who's who" of Taos: Padre Martínez, priest, publisher and politician; Captain Smith H. Simpson, Carson's confidential secretary; Teresina Bent Scheurich, daughter of Governor Bent; Ralph Meyers, Indian trader and artist; and Mabel Dodge Luhan, the art patroness and philanthropist. Also many leading Taos families have burial plots in the *camposanto*: Santistevan and Martínez as well as Dolan and Liebert, merchants who arrived in the 19th century and whose descendants are still active in the community and its vibrant social life.

Just inside the entrance to the cemetery is the gravestone of one Arthur Rochford Manby, the land swindler whose beheaded body was found on July 4, 1929, in his home on Pueblo Road. Leaving the resting place of Taos heroes and heroines, one walks through the "Artist's Grove," a stand of aspens dedicated to the original members of the Taos Society of Artists.

In this *camposanto* near the entrance to Taos Pueblo, with a splendid view of Taos Mountain through groves of cottonwood and spruce trees, lie buried four of the original charter members of the Taos Society of Artists. This talented quartet made a reputation across the nation and around the world for Taos as a source for American works of art. They are Oscar E. Berninghaus, Eanger Irving Couse, Victor Higgins and Bert Geer Phillips. Known as the "pioneer painter," Phillips was the first Anglo artist to set up his permanent studio in Taos and spend the rest of his life painting the Pueblo Indians.

The Couse gravestone is a smooth, perfectly round, beautifully grained brown granite boulder on which the name "COUSE" is chiseled in bold, block letters. Mantled with shiny green ivy in the warm summer months, the massive stone, selected by Couse's grandchildren, is a work of art in itself and a marvelous memorial to a rare talent.

The Victor Higgins gravestone, an abstract sculpture of rose granite, makes for a fitting monument to a talented artist who had strong impressionistic leanings. Oscar Berninghaus from St. Louis and Bert Phillips, the "pioneer painter," lie buried next to their wives, Winifred and Rose, respectively. Other prominent *Taoseños* lying at rest here are the lovely Blanche Chloe Grant, whose headstone is engraved "Historian of Taos"; Dr. Fred Muller, a highly respected Taos physician; and William Hinde, who ran the blacksmith shop where New York artist Ernest L. Blumenschein brought the broken wagon wheel to be repaired and thus began the flourishing Taos Art Colony. The visitor leaves the quiet *camposanto* with the feeling that these outstanding artists, who after a lifetime of hard work at their paint-splattered easels on mountaintops and *mesas* or in their artifact-filled skylit studios, deserve an eternity of peaceful sleep.

Parts of this quaint old building, originally the residence of the prominent Taos trader, Carlos Beaubien, date back to the early 1800s. In the early years of the 20th century, the house was purchased by Ralph Meyers (1885-1948), who was a painter, silversmith, wood carver, Spanish-Colonial furniture maker, weaver and vegetable dye maker for his own fabrics. He knew, as well as the Indians, how to fashion moccasins from buckskin, which they scraped and bleached with sheep's brains to a snowy whiteness. Being a close and trusted friend of the Taos Pueblo Indians, Meyers became an Indian trader and opened The Mission Shop, the oldest trading post in Taos. He and his beautiful wife, Rowena, went on to become the central figures in Taos during those days before the valley was discovered by the rest of the world. Over the years, many celebrities visited the shop, which later was named *El Rincón* (The Corner). Among the notables were Leopold Stowkowski, Gloria Vanderbilt and Lucille Ball, to name a few. Blonde, beauteous Millicent Rogers was a frequent customer, arriving in worn blue jeans, a starched white blouse with puffed sleeves and lots of Indian jewelry on her neck and wrists. Next door to the trading post was the famous La Doña Luz Restaurant located on the site of the residence of Doña Luz Martínez y Lucero, a famous *Taoseña* of yesteryear. The *cantina*, originally run by "Frenchie" Hutton, then by Jim Griffin, was a favorite haunt of Lady Dorothy Brett, who would not be without her trusty hearing aid. One day,

while a waiter was mumbling the menu of the day into Dorothy's ear, she exclaimed, "Young man, speak to my bosom. That's where the batteries are!" After Ralph Meyers' death in 1948, Rowena ran the trading post. Her daughter, Nina, has recently taken over the reins of the shop and the museum, which displays such interesting artifacts as Kit Carson's buckskin trousers, a Ute Indian cradle and the oldest Holy Water font in New Mexico. El Rincón Trading Post is located on the south side of Kit Carson Road just a stone's throw from Pueblo Road and Taos Plaza.

Founded in 1947, the Taos Book Shop was run for a quarter of a century by co-owners Claire Morrill and Genevieve Janssen. Its nooks and crannies have served as a rendezvous for *Taoseños* and travelers searching for out-of-print books about the great Southwest. After two earlier locations on the plaza and in the Mission Shop, the two "bookstore girls" moved to the present site next to the Cafe Tazza on Kit Carson Road.

The old adobe once belonged to the talented artist Victor Higgins, who made a reputation for capturing the landscape of northern New Mexico in his impressionistic watercolors and oil paintings. When Claire Morrill left her job in 1947 as managing editor of a Michigan newspaper and was about to set up the book shop in Taos, she told her friends, "We might very well lose our shirts, but we'll have a helluva lot of fun doing it." Their clerical assistants from the start were two Taos Pueblo Indians, John Andres Romero and Luis Suazo, both skilled moccasin makers.

The only customer to enjoy curbside service was Mabel Dodge. Her chauffeur came into the shop once a week to say, "Mrs. Luhan is here." An earlier telephone call alerted the "girls" to Mabel's arrival; they would then take a selection of novels and nonfiction books to the big black Buick where she chose what she wanted.

In those days the Taos Book Shop was the only one in the country where one could find a scarce item of Western Americana from a clerk, who, though he spoke three languages, still could not read or write. Claire Morrill's delightful book, *A Taos Mosaic*, in which she captured the unique quality of the frontier town and its colorful inhabitants, remains high on the waiting list at the Harwood Library even today. Other well-stocked bookstores in Taos not to be missed include The Brodsky Bookshop, Merlin's Garden, Moby Dickens Bookshop, Fernando de Taos on the Plaza, and Ten Directions Books. All are unique in their own way!

Tradition tells *Taoseños* that the wall of the El Patio Restaurant remains as the oldest adobe structure in town. Apparently, the wall was part of two rooms originally built by Taos Pueblo Indians to serve as an outpost along the old Chihauhua Trail. In one of the many skirmishes that took place in Taos, the building was partially destroyed but was rebuilt and occupied by the Spanish government from the 17th to the 19th century. In 1846, the dwelling became the office of Charles Bent, the first U.S. Territorial Governor of New Mexico. Bent was assassinated in the Rebellion of 1847, but the structure remained in the hands of his family for several years. Kit Carson and Buffalo Bill Cody, the white-bearded hero of his own Wild West Show, were frequent visitors here in their search for the "good life" to be enjoyed in Taos. It was Carson who once remarked, "Who has seen the women, heard the bells, or smelled the *piñón* smoke of Taos will never be able to leave."

Decades later, in 1944, El Patio opened its doors as a highly regarded restaurant in the ancient adobe building. Since then it has remained a favorite dining place for locals, visitors and celebrities alike. Quite a few people in Taos, especially the writer Blanche Grant, believed that the word "Taos" comes from the Chinese word "Tao." As a result, back in the 1980s, a group of imaginative artists opened a gallery at the end of narrow Teresina Lane next to the "Old Taos" antique shop and added the oriental-style architectural effects to the off-beat building. Today, El Patio's "oldest wall" is connected to the "Chinese Wall," thus adding another delightful dimension to the ambiance of Taos.

Dodge pick-ups in various states of disrepair delivering just-harvested purple-blossomed alfalfa; Fords packing piles of newly chopped firewood finding their way over wavy washboard roads; Chevies shuffling over rusty cattle guards, *mesas* and *arroyos*—all of these *Taoseño*-driven dilapidated vehicles have one wonderful thing in common: a big dog in the back! Canines of all kinds—pedigrees and Heinz 57 varieties, retrievers, setters and spaniels, siberian huskies and malamutes—all look out searchingly from the back of the pick-up to drink in the panorama of the Taos Valley landscape. They inhale the *piñón*-scented, pure mountain air and check to see who among Taos's many famous residents are strolling and shopping along Pueblo Road and the Raton Highway. Each one of these lovable pets feels right at home, for the rear platform of the mud-splattered truck is the home-away-from-home where it was weaned and raised as a puppy. As a matter of fact, the dog would be adrift like a ship in a storm if it weren't safely within the truck's pitted steel embrace. Whether a St. Bernard or a boxer, a greyhound or a German shepherd, a great Dane or a chow, it's a dog's life in the Town of Taos, New Mexico!

Historic Taos has been a magnetic trading post for centuries well before Coronado's conquistadores arrived from Spain. The Spanish soon discovered that the trade fairs, or rendezvous where numerous Indian tribes exchanged goods such as exotic seashells, dried meats and thick buffalo hides, were the place to be. Later, bearded, ruddy French trappers descended with their guns into the Taos Valley with precious furs and beaver pelts. They were joined by industrious German immigrants who journeyed to the Southwest over the Santa Fe Trail to establish their thriving mercantile stores. So how did a new arrival spell the name of this captivating village where Pueblo Indians, Apaches, Comanches, Spaniards, French, German and the artistic Anglos congregated? The list went from Tua-Tah to Tasoo, from Taox to Tasoo, and from Taco to Tugs. Over the years bicyclists from Boulder, photographers from Philadelphia, newswriters from New York and big-wigs from Boston all have contributed their mistakes to the melange of words. A sign in Randall's Hardware Store on Paseo del Pueblo Sur proudly displays "The Different Ways to Spell Taos." The board starts with Taus and ends with Tas. So the curtain falls on the tumultuous tale of legendary Taos.

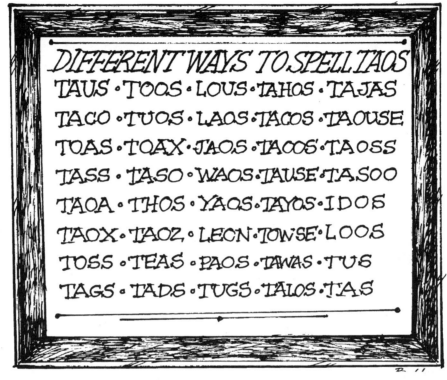

DIFFERENT WAYS TO SPELL TAOS

TAUS • TOOS • LOUS • TAHOS • TAJAS
TACO • TUOS • LAOS • TACOS • TAOUSE
TOAS • TOAX • JAOS • TACOS • TAOSS
TASS • TASO • WAOS • TAUSE • TASOO
TAOA • THOS • YAOS • TAYOS • IDOS
TAOX • TAOZ • LECN • TOWSE • LOOS
TOSS • TEAS • PAOS • TAWAS • TUS
TAGS • TADS • TUGS • TALOS • TAS

Bibliography

Bickerstaff, Laura. *Pioneer Artists of Taos*,
Old West Publications Co., 1983.

Blumenschein, Helen. *Sounds & Lights of Taos Valley*,
Deckerhoff's, 1983.

Broder, Patricia Janis. *Taos, A Painter's Dream*,
Little Brown, 1980.

Bunting, Bainbridge. *Taos Adobes: The Spanish Colonial and Territorial Architecture of the Taos Valley*,
University of New Mexico Press, 1964.

Campa, Arthur L. *Hispanic Culture in the Southwest*,
University of Oklahoma Press, 1978.

Cather, Willa. *Death Comes for the Archbishop*,
Alfred A. Knopf, 1927.

Estergreen, M. Morgan. *Kit Carson: A Portrait in Courage*,
Norman: University of Okalahoma Press, 1962.

Evans, Max. *"Long" John Dunn of Taos*,
Clearlight Publishers, Revised 1993

Florin, Lambert. *Ghost Towns of the Southwest*,
Promontory Point Press, 1970-71.

Foster, Joseph. *D.H. Lawrence in Taos*,
University of New Mexico Press, 1972.

Garrard, Lewis H. *Wah-toyah & the Taos Trail*,
University of Oklahoma Press, 1955.

Grant, Blanche C. *When Old Trails Were New, The Story of Taos*,
Press of the Pioneers, 1934.

James, Rebecca Salsbury. *Allow Me To Present 18 Ladies & Gentlemen of Taos*, NM, 1885-1939, El Crepúsculo, 1953.

Keegan, Marcia. *Taos Pueblo & Its Sacred Blue Lake*,
Clear Light Publishers, 1991.

Lawrence, Frieda. *Not I, But the Wind*, Rydal Press, 1934.

Luhan, Mabel Dodge. *Lorenzo in Taos*, M. Secker, 1932.

Morrill, Claire A. *Taos Mosaic, Portrait of a New Mexico Village*,
University of New Mexico Press, 1973.

Nichols, John. *The Milgro Beanfield War*,
Holt-Rinehart and Winston, 1974.

Peters, Steve. *Headless in Taos, Arthur Rochford Manby*, 1972

Richards, Rick. *Ski Pioneers: Ernie Blake, His Friends, and the Making of Taos Ski Valley*, 1992.

Sherman, James E. *Ghost Towns and Mining Camps of New Mexico*, Norman: University of Oklahoma Press, 1975.

Sherman, John. *Taos: A Pictorial History*, William Gannon, 1990.

Sloane, Eric. *Return to Taos, A Twice Told Tale*, W. Funk, 1982.

Taggett, Sherry Clayton. *Paintbrushes & Pistols, How the Taos Artists Sold the West*, J. Muir Publications, 1990,

Weber, David J. *The Taos Trappers, The Fur Trade from New Mexico*, University of Oklahoma Press, 1971.

About the Author

BILL HEMP was born May 3, 1928, in St. Louis, Missouri and raised in Philadelphia, where he graduated from St. Joseph's University in 1950. His career in advertising and public relations spanned 36 years working at N.W. Ayer, Young & Rubicam and serving as Creative Director for 15 years with Burson-Marsteller in New York City until his retirement in 1992.

After serving with the U.S. Sixth Fleet in the Mediterranean during the Korean Conflict, he hiked around the world for two years exploring and sketching in 35 countries from Ireland to Japan. After living in Manhattan, Hemp and his wife, Maggie, settled in Point Lookout, Long Island, where they raised their sons, Bill Jr., Brendan, Joseph and Christopher.

Pursuing his love of art, he took courses at the Salmagundi Club in Manhattan, the old haunt of Taos Society of Artists painters Ernest Blumenschein and Bert Geer Phillips, and won a prize for his pen-and-inks in the Greenwich Village Outdoor Art Exhibit. He is the author/illustrator of two other books, *New York Enclaves* and *If Ever You Go to Dublin Town*. Over the past two years he has been illustrating in pen and ink and writing about the Taos Valley, speaking with the diverse townspeople, exploring the sun-splashed pueblo and plazas and gathering material for *Taos Landmarks & Legends*. Bill and Maggie reside in Taos Cañon in the shadow of the Sangre de Cristo Mountains.

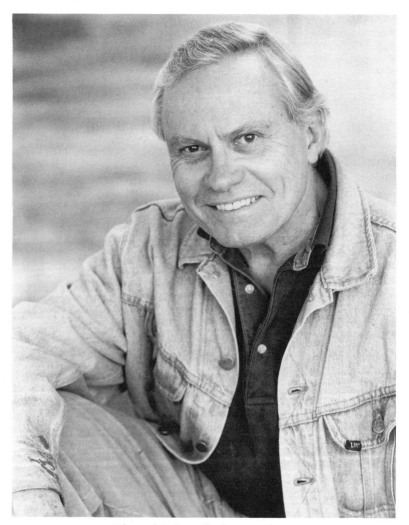

(Photo: Christian Pollard, New York, NY)

Index